THE DICTIONARY OF

Folklore

David Adams Leeming, Ph.D.
University of Connecticut

Professor Emeritus

General Editor

Marilee Foglesong
Former Young Adult Coordinator, New York Public Library

Adviser

Franklin Watts

A Division of Scholastic Inc.

New York   Toronto   London   Auckland   Sydney

Mexico City   New Delhi   Hong Kong

Danbury, Connecticut

DEVELOPED, DESIGNED, AND PRODUCED BY
BOOK BUILDERS LLC

Library of Congress Cataloging-in-Publication Data

The dictionary of folklore / David Adams Leeming, general editor.
    p. cm.
    Includes bibliographical references and index.
    ISBN 0-531-11985-8
    1. Folklore—Dictionaries, Juvenile. [1. Folklore—Dictionaries.] I. Leeming, David Adams, 1937–

GR69 .D53 2002
398'.03—dc21   2001022034

Contents

Note to the Reader

If you have ever played the game "Telephone," you will have some idea of what folklore is. Folklore is passed down orally (by word of mouth) from one generation to the next and from one country to another. As folklore travels, it sometimes changes, so when a story finally gets written, it is different in different places. Cinderella, for instance, is told one way in China and another way in France.

There are many kinds of folklore. Myths, superstitions, nursery rhymes, folk songs, legends, fairy tales, tall tales, fables, game rhymes, and riddles are all forms of folklore that have been passed down through the ages. Parents and grandparents tell stories to children, or children entertain each other with tales on playgrounds, at home, or at school. Because all of us are "folk," this *Dictionary of Folklore* can help us understand ourselves and one another better.

How to Use This Book

Each term discussed in the dictionary appears in dark type in alphabetical order. Look up both **Fairy Tale** and **The Fisherman and His Wife** under *F*. Some definitions, or entries, contain words in SMALL CAPITAL LETTERS. For example, the entry **Aesop** begins by saying, "The most famous teller of the FABLE" and ends with, "[*See also* KIPLING, RUDYARD; PANCHATANTRA.]" The SMALL CAPITAL LETTERS, or cross-references, mean that you can find more information about Aesop and fables in other entries in the book.

In addition to the alphabetical entries, this dictionary includes special features in lightly colored boxes. For example, see the entry **Ballad and Folk Song** and the nearby box titled *A Folk Song:* "Go Down, Moses," which contains an example of a folk song. Near the entry **Cinderella** is a feature about Aschenputtel. At the back of the book, the index will help you locate topics, and the Selected Bibliography lists other books that will help with research and pleasure reading.

Note to the Educator

The Dictionary of Folklore is a resource book of folklore that introduces a wide range of topics, including ballads and folk songs, Bible stories, fables, fairy tales, folktales, game rhymes, legends, myths, parables, riddles, and tall tales. There are also examples of what might be called "literary folklore," stories told in a folkloric style by established writers such as Mark Twain. Entries include examples of the above as well as a large selection of important characters and collections.

Although the various kinds of folklore are treated as separate entities, what is a myth to one person is a sacred story to another. The distinction between myth and simple folktale is sometimes unclear. Tall tales and legends, too, are often hard to distinguish from each other, because they share the quality of exaggeration.

Four types of features supplement the entries. One type illustrates a specific kind of folklore; for example, see *A Folk Song:* "Go Down, Moses" accompanying **Ballad and Folk Song.** Another type illustrates an archetypal character, such as the one near the entry **Wicked Stepmother.** A third type of feature, such as the one near **Kipling, Rudyard,** shows the work of a collector or writer. The fourth presents a variant version of a popular tale; for example, near **Little Red Riding Hood** appears a brief retelling of a similar Chinese story.

Folklore is, of course, common to all cultures, and the editors have recognized this fact in their selections. The emphasis in this book is on American folklore, which develops from the traditions of American Indians, European Americans, African Americans, Asian Americans, and other groups who have settled on the North American continent. We hope that this dictionary will help young readers further explore American folklore, as well as develop their interest in other cultures and regions.

David Adams Leeming, *General Editor*

Abraham Lincoln as "Honest Abe"

Abraham Lincoln as "Honest Abe" ❧ The sixteenth president of the United States. Abraham Lincoln (1809–1865) became president in spite of many obstacles. His father was a poor farmer who drifted from place to place along the American frontier. As a child, Lincoln did not go to school. He grew up to be an awkward, homely man who looked as if his clothes did not fit him.

Lincoln became a popular president for many reasons, including his reputation for complete honesty. This reputation earned him the nickname "Honest Abe." Stories about his honesty became part of the folklore surrounding him, and some have been turned into LEGEND. These stories tell, for instance, of Lincoln as a young man working in a store. In one story, Lincoln added up a customer's bill again after she left the store and discovered that he had charged her six cents too much. After the store closed for the day, he walked nearly three miles to return the customer's six cents. In another story, Lincoln weighed a half-pound of tea for a

This photograph of Lincoln was taken during his presidency.

customer. The next morning, he discovered that an extra weight was on the scale, and he had accidentally charged the customer for four extra ounces of tea. Honest Abe weighed four ounces of tea, closed the shop, and took it to the customer.

Adam and Eve ❧ The first humans God created, according to the Bible. The story of Adam and Eve is told in the Book of Genesis, which is the first book of the Bible. It is one of many BIBLE STORIES important to Jews and Christians, for it is part of a larger story that describes the creation of the world. Even people who have not read the Bible are likely to know the story of Adam and Eve.

The Story. According to Genesis, Adam and Eve were the first humans God created. God wanted them to fill the earth with people and to "have dominion over," or rule over, the creatures of the earth. God put Adam and Eve in the Garden of Eden, a paradise where they had everything they needed. God told them that they could eat the fruit of any tree in the garden except the Tree of the Knowledge of Good and Evil. Satan, or the devil, appeared in the garden in the form of a snake and persuaded Eve to eat from the forbidden tree. Eve then persuaded Adam to do the same. Adam and Eve knew that they had broken God's law, and they tried to hide. God found Adam and Eve and made them leave the Garden of Eden. He said that they and all humans who came after them would have to suffer pain and die.

Men and Women. For many centuries, the story of Adam and Eve has sometimes made it hard for men and women to get along as equals. The second chapter of Genesis says that God created Eve from one of Adam's ribs to be a "helpmeet," or a helper, to him. Some people unfairly believe that because of Eve's position as Adam's helper and her disobedience to God, women are weak and not as good as men. [*See also* SACRED STORY.]

Aesop ❧ The most famous teller of the FABLE, a short tale that teaches a lesson. Many people think Aesop was a Greek slave who lived during the seventh century B.C.E. The world will never know if one storyteller named Aesop really lived. It is possible that many different people, whose names are now lost, made up stories that much later were all said to be by Aesop.

The fables began as spoken stories. Then they were written down in Greek and later in Latin. As the centuries went by, the fables were translated into other languages.

The lesson that a fable teaches is called its moral. Sometimes a fable states the moral in the form of a PROVERB. For example, in the fable called "The Fox and the Grapes," a fox that cannot reach delicious-looking grapes suddenly decides that the grapes must taste sour, so the moral is given as "It is easy to despise what you cannot get."

The animals in Aesop's fables stand for human beings. So the fox might represent a greedy person who cannot get what he or she wants. [*See also* KIPLING, RUDYARD; PANCHATANTRA.]

African American Folklore 🦋

All the stories, songs, and sayings originally told and sung by early African Americans and passed down from one generation to another. African Americans have a rich folklore tradition. Many of the themes and characters come from Africa.

Examples include such character types as TRICKSTERS, GHOSTS AND GOBLINS, and animals.

In the New World, the first African Americans were enslaved, so most did not know how to read or write. For this reason, most African American folklore was not written down but was passed orally from one generation to the next. Because storytellers did not always remember exactly what they had heard, the stories sometimes changed from one storyteller to another. People told stories out loud, making up parts as they went along, so that the stories came out sounding less formal than if they had been written down in a book. Also, storytellers sometimes imitated the way preachers spoke when they recited stories from the Bible.

Collections of African American Folklore. African American folklore became popular in 1867 when a book called *Slave Songs of the United States* was published. Many Americans became interested in the songs, often called Negro spirituals, that slaves sang to keep their spirits up when

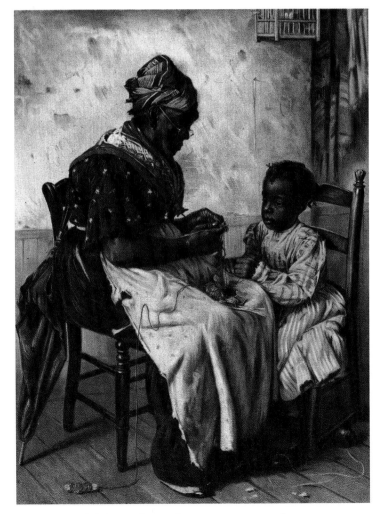

An older African American woman and a young girl sewing—and maybe sharing stories.

they were working. Another book that made African American folklore popular was *Uncle Remus: His Songs and Sayings*, written by Joel Chandler Harris and published in 1880. This book contains many animal stories. One of the best-known characters from these stories is Brer Rabbit (*see* BRER RABBIT AND TAR BABY), a trickster who uses his wits to outsmart Brer Fox, Brer Wolf, and Brer Bear. About the same time, storytellers began to spread the fame of JOHN HENRY, a heroic railroad worker who could drive steel spikes into the ground faster than a machine (*see* JOHN HENRY'S HAMMER). More recently, writers Langston Hughes and Arna Bontemps gathered African American stories in *The Book of Negro Folklore*, published in 1958. These are only a few of the many collections of African American folklore. Some of these stories tell of the struggles of African Americans, but many are filled with humor and fun. [*See also* FOLKTALE; BALLAD AND FOLK SONG.]

Aladdin ❧ *See* MAGIC OBJECTS AND WIZARDS.

Ali Baba and the Forty Thieves ❧

A story from ONE THOUSAND AND ONE NIGHTS. The *One Thousand and One Nights* is an ancient story collection of romances, fairy tales, legends, and parables. (*see* FAIRY TALE; LEGEND; PARABLE). The narrator, who is a woman named Scheherazade, tells one story each night to entertain her husband, the king, to keep him from killing her. Each night, she stops just before the end of the story, so that the King must keep her alive until the next night to hear the ending; but then Scheherazade begins a new story. No one knows who originally wrote the stories in this collection. They came from many different countries, including Iran, Iraq, India, Egypt, and Turkey. Many of the stories, including those about Sinbad the Sailor and Aladdin, are well known around the world.

"Ali Baba and the Forty Thieves" did not appear in the original collection. A French writer named Antoine Galland added it later when he translated the collection into French.

The Story. One day Ali Baba, a poor woodcutter, watched a band of thieves enter a cave filled with treasures by saying the magic words "Open Sesame." After the robbers left, he used the same magic words to enter the cave. He then took six bags of gold coins. Ali Baba offered to share his money with his brother Kassim, but Kassim insisted on going to the cave himself. The thieves caught Kassim and killed him.

Later, the thieves found Ali Baba. Their leader disguised himself as an oil merchant and asked Ali Baba to let him stay for a night. The other thieves were hiding in large oil jars that were supposedly going to the market. But Morgiana, a servant girl, discovered the thieves and killed them by pouring boiling oil into the jars. Later she killed the leader. Morgiana married Ali Baba's son, and the family enjoyed the treasure from the thieves' cave.

American Indian Folklore ❧ The stories and other forms of art, such as music and dancing, that belong to the people who lived in the Americas before people from Europe arrived. The kinds of stories include MYTH, FOLKTALE, and LEGEND.

American Indian Myths. Each tribe has its own myths, but they all tell about the same things. For instance, all the tribes have myths to explain where the world came from and how people got here, although they use different words and different names for characters. See, for example, "Seneca Earth Diver." The tribes also have myths about powerful, supernatural heroes (*see* HEROES OR HEROINES) who fight monsters. See, for example, GLOOSCAP SLAYS THE MONSTER. In these myths, both the heroes and the monsters can change their shapes to try to fool each other.

Other myths that are popular with the different American Indian tribes tell about war, love, animals, ghosts (*see* GHOSTS AND GOBLINS),

An example of American Indian folklore, a Cheyenne doll.

and death. Many of the myths have characters known as TRICKSTERS. As the word suggests, a trickster plays tricks and pranks. But a trickster can also help people by making good things happen.

In general, myths deal with many important things. Therefore, people think of myths as religious. By telling how people once lived and by showing who is rewarded and who is punished, myths teach people how to behave and how not to behave.

American Indian Folktales and Legends. Folktales and legends have a different purpose than myths. Whereas myths teach people lessons, folktales and legends entertain people. These stories make listeners and readers feel good about their ancestors, the people who came before them. Sometimes listeners and readers even laugh about what happened a long time ago. An example of an American Indian folktale is HOW ANTELOPE CARRIER SAVED THE THUNDERBIRDS AND BECAME CHIEF OF THE WINGED CREATURES, and an example of an American Indian legend is ONEIDA MAIDEN SAVIOR.

Ananse ❧ *See* TRICKSTERS.

Andersen, Hans Christian (1805–1875)

❧ Hans Christian Andersen was an author from Denmark. As a child, he was poor and received little schooling, but when he grew up, he wrote poems, novels, and plays. He is best remembered, though, for writing more than 150 FAIRY TALES. Many of these fairy tales are still popular throughout the world. Well-known titles include "The Princess and the Pea," "The Emperor's New Clothes," "The Little Mermaid," and "The Ugly Duckling." In his fairy tales, Andersen stressed kindness and sympathy, especially for outsiders, possibly because as a teenager he was bullied at school by other boys and the school's headmaster. [*See also* LITERARY FOLKTALE; THE NIGHTINGALE.]

Annie Oakley and Her Gun

❧ A LEGEND about a character from the American Old West known for her talent for straight shooting. One of the most famous names in American folklore is Annie Oakley. She was born Phoebe Anne Oakley Mozee in Ohio in 1860. People called her "Little Sure Shot," because it was said that, at the age of eight, she could shoot the head off of a running quail.

Annie Oakley used her incredible ability to shoot straight during her 17 years as a star of Buffalo Bill's Wild West show. During her performances, Annie shot corks out of bottles and the flames off candles. She could hit the edge of a playing card from 30 steps away, and she often shot holes in playing cards that were flipped into the air. At that time, free tickets (to a baseball game, for example) had similar holes in them, so the tickets were often called "Annie Oakleys."

Annie Oakley died in 1926. In 1946, she became the subject of a famous musical comedy, *Annie Get Your Gun.* [*See also* CALAMITY JANE; SHOOT-OUT AT THE OK CORRAL.]

Arabian Nights ❧ *See* ONE THOUSAND AND ONE NIGHTS.

Baba Yaga Tale

Baba Yaga Tale ❧ A FOLKTALE about an old woman who often appears in Russian folklore. In some tales, she is a kind and wise old woman, and in others, she is a mean stepmother or a wicked fairy godmother. Baba Yaga usually lives in the forest in a hut that stands on hens' legs. The fence surrounding her house is made of human bones. Atop the fence are human skulls with glaring eyes. Usually, she is as thin as a skeleton, so she is sometimes called *Baba Yaga Bony Leg*. She has a long nose, and her long, sharp teeth are made of iron, making it easy for her to eat children. Russian parents sometimes tell their children that Baba Yaga eats only children who do not behave.

One Version of the Story. A merchant's wife died, and the merchant married a woman he hoped would be a mother to his daughter, Lubachka. But the stepmother hated Lubachka, so she ordered Lubachka into the forest to fetch a needle from her sister. Lubachka's aunt, though, told her that the stepmother was really sending her to Baba Yaga. The aunt gave Lubachka everything she needed to survive: a red ribbon, a bottle of oil, a loaf of bread, and a piece of ham.

When Lubachka arrived at Baba Yaga's house, she knew that she had to act fast to keep from

This illustration of a very thin woman with a long nose matches the description of Baba Yaga.

being eaten. She used the ham to bribe Baba Yaga's cat to give her a magical comb and kerchief that would help her escape. The bread kept Baba Yaga's dogs from chasing her. The oil helped her get the gate open. She used the red ribbon to tie together the trees that tried to grab her. The comb and the kerchief kept Baba Yaga from catching Lubachka by turning into a thick forest and a river. When Lubachka returned home, she told her father what had happened. Her father then chased the WICKED STEPMOTHER into the woods, where she was eaten by wolves. Lubachka and her father lived happily ever after. [*See also* FAIRY TALE; CINDERELLA.]

The Baker's Dozen ✤ A FOLKTALE

that explains the origin of the baker's dozen—a dozen items with one added. Long ago, people took their baked goods seriously. After all, a family's whole meal might be a loaf of bread. Unfortunately, some bakers cheated their customers. A dishonest baker might sell a 14-ounce loaf bread for the price of a full pound, or 16 ounces. As long ago as the time of the pharaohs in Egypt, there were serious punishments for dishonest bakers. Some were nailed by their ears to the doors of their shops for selling loaves of bread that weighed less than they should. Eventually, bakers

Old-fashioned bakers show their baked goods.

began adding an extra amount to an order so they could never be accused of giving too little. Many experts believe this practice explains the origin of the baker's dozen—13 items instead of 12.

Another Explanation. An American folktale provides another explanation for the practice of adding a thirteenth cookie or muffin to a dozen. Many years ago, when New York was still a Dutch colony, there was a baker nicknamed Baas, who made the best cookies for miles around. One day an old woman entered his shop and asked for a dozen cookies. Baas counted out 12 cookies, but the old woman demanded an additional cookie, saying "I want a dozen!" Baas replied that he had counted out a dozen, but the old woman paid no attention to him. She kept demanding a dozen. Finally, Baas lost all patience and told the woman that if she wanted another cookie, she should go to the devil for it.

The old woman left the shop, but some very strange things began to happen. Cookies disappeared, and loaves of bread rose into the air and flew up the chimney. Then bad luck came to Baas's wife and children. In desperation, Baas prayed to Saint Nicholas, who appeared to the baker and advised him to give the old woman what she wanted.

The next time the old woman came to the shop to buy a dozen cookies, Baas gave her 13 cookies instead of 12. "The spell is broken," she said. "Remember this day. From now on a dozen is 13. It shall be known as a baker's dozen."

Ballad and Folk Song

Oral stories or emotional expressions made up by anonymous people and told musically rather than in only a spoken way. The term *folk song* is more general than the term *ballad*. Usually, no one knows who wrote a folk song, because most folk songs have been passed down orally from generation to generation. A folk song remains popular because it expresses the beliefs, longings, or sufferings of many people in the culture. Because they were not originally written down, folk songs changed over time,

and new singers altered the melodies or words.

A good example of a folk song from the African American culture is "Go Down, Moses." The accompanying feature gives some of the lyrics of this song. Like most folk songs, "Go Down, Moses" is written in stanzas and has a repeated refrain, and the music and language are simple. ("Go Down, Moses" and other folk songs that deal with bondage on Earth and a belief in future freedom are also called *spirituals*.)

A ballad is a type of folk song. Many ballads tell stories about love, death, war, and other dramatic or historical events. Although some ballads are funny, most are sad. Like much folk literature, ballads rely on familiar plots and characters and repeated words and phrases to help people remember them.

Many ballads have a familiar structure and meter: a line with four beats followed by a line with three beats and then four-beat and three-beat lines. The second and fourth lines almost always rhyme. Here is the opening stanza from an old English ballad called "The Wife of Usher's Well."

There lived a wife at Usher's
    Well,
And a wealthy wife was she;
She had three stout and
    stalwart sons,
And sent them o'er the sea.

A Folk Song: "Go Down, Moses"

Here are a few verses and the chorus of an African American folk song known as a *spiritual*. Many spirituals had double meanings. This song tells the biblical story of the Israelites escaping slavery in Egypt. When African American slaves sang the song in the nineteenth century, they were looking forward to their own release from bondage.

When Israel was in Egypt land,
Let my people go!
Oppressed so hard they could not
    stand,
Let my people go!

Chorus
Go down, Moses,
Way down in Egypt land.
Tell ole Pharaoh,
Let my people go!

Thus say the Lord, bold Moses
    said,
Let my people go!
If not I'll smite your first-born
    dead,
Let my people go!

Chorus

No more shall they in bondage
    toil,
Let my people go!
Let them come out with Egypt's
    spoil,
Let my people go!

Chorus

Some ballads are called *literary ballads*. This term refers to ballads that did not begin as part of an oral tradition. They were composed by poets to imitate traditional oral ballads. Authors who wrote famous literary ballads include John Keats and Samuel Taylor Coleridge in the late eighteenth century and the early nineteenth century. In the modern world, many popular singers and songwriters, especially writers of country-and-western songs, carry on the traditions of ballads and folk songs. [*See also* CLEMENTINE; FRANKIE AND JOHNNY; JOHN HENRY'S HAMMER; STREETS OF LAREDO; TSIMSHIAN LULLABY; YANKEE DOODLE.]

Bards, Other Storytellers ❦

People who tell stories, sing songs, or recite long poems, usually about heroic deeds. These long poems, called *epics*, tell stories about kings, warriors, and other heroes (*see* HEROES OR HEROINES). Examples of ancient bards include those who recited the Greek epics of Homer, telling of heroes of the Trojan war (*see* TROJAN HORSE). Some bards played harps or other instruments as they recited their tales.

Some of the ancient bards of the British Isles and Europe were very famous. They performed for wealthy people and were very highly paid. Their stories and songs told about

An ancient British bard and his harp.

heroic and noble deeds. Bards who were not so rich or famous traveled about the countryside telling their stories to anyone who would listen. These bards usually sang popular folk songs instead of telling stories about kings and heroes.

Other Storytellers. Professional storytellers were popular in other cultures as well. In western Africa, they were called *griots*. In Arabic countries, they were called *hakawtis*. In ancient Greece, they were called *rhapsodes*. The Anglo-Saxon tribes of Europe called them *scops*. Americans Indian tribes also had storytellers who passed on the wisdom of their ancestors. All of these artists were respected members of their communities, because the people believed that storytellers got their wisdom from a higher power or god.

Bear Fishes through Ice with Tail ❧ A TALL TALE told by American Indians to explain why bears have short tails. We are told that before the events of this story took place, bears' tails were long.

One day Bear was hungry and asked Fox to share the fish he was eating. Fox explained that he had only enough for himself. But Fox told Bear that he would show him how to catch his own fish. So Fox went out on the ice and sat near a hole, dangling his tail into the water. He explained to Bear that the crawfish would catch onto his tail, and then there would be fish for dinner. The more his tail pinched, the more crawfish there would be.

So Bear put his tail down the hole in the ice. Soon he felt his tail pinching, but he wanted to catch a lot of fish, so he kept his tail in the freezing water. Finally, when he tried to stand up, he couldn't move. He turned to see that his tail was frozen into the ice. Fox had tricked him; there were no crawfish, and the pinching was from ice freezing around his tail. So Bear pulled to free himself and tore his tail off. Only a stump remained.

Beauty and the Beast ❧ A European FAIRY TALE or FOLKTALE that tells of the love between a beautiful young woman and an enchanted beast who is changed back into a prince (*see* PRINCES OR PRINCESSES)

Walter Crane (1845–1915) was a very famous illustrator. Here is a scene he did for "Beauty and the Beast."

by her love. The theme of beauty and the beast runs through the folklore of Europe. The most familiar version of the story tells of a poor merchant whose daughters ask for presents when he goes on a trip.

The Story. The merchant's two older daughters asked for expensive presents, but the youngest daughter, Beauty, asked only for a rose. When the merchant stopped at a garden to pick a rose for her, the beast, who owned the garden, accused him of stealing. The beast gave the merchant a choice: to give up either his life or one of his daugh-ters. To save her father's life, Beauty went to live with the beast. Over time, she became fond of him. One day she thought he had died, and she confessed her love for him. This confession broke a spell, and the beast changed into a handsome prince. The two married and lived happily ever after.

Other Versions. In some versions of the story, the roles are reversed. A handsome knight breaks a spell that has turned a beautiful woman into an ugly hag, often called a "loathly lady."

The Theme in Recent Times. The theme became common in later works of literature. For example, in Charlotte Brontë's novel *Jane Eyre*, Jane's love transforms the gruff, homely Rochester into a loving hus-band. The theme also appears in ro-mance novels in which a beautiful heroine (*see* HEROES OR HEROINES) draws out a man's "princely" virtues. Moviemakers use the theme as well. One good example is *King Kong*. In this movie, a beautiful actress is cap-tured by a gigantic ape that wins the sympathy of the audience by treat-ing the actress with kindness and love.

Bible Stories ❧ Stories from the Jewish-Christian Bible that have be-come part of folklore. These are stories that many people know even if they do not read the Bible. The

David attacks Goliath.

stories have become part of folklore, because they contain ideas that are important for everyone.

Many Bible stories come from the Old Testament of the Bible. Examples include the stories of ADAM AND EVE in the Garden of Eden, NOAH'S FLOOD, David and Goliath, and Jonah and the whale. Others come from the New Testament, including the PARABLE of the Prodigal Son. Many phrases common in the English language come from Bible stories. A sports announcer, for example, might refer to two players or teams as "David and Goliath," the underdog being David and the favorite being Goliath. Similarly, a

A Bible Story: "David Defeats Goliath"

This is a legendary story about a small boy named David who defeats a giant warrior named Goliath.

The Philistine warrior Goliath, who was nine feet and nine inches tall, offered a challenge to the Israelites for 40 days. Goliath's challenge was that if the Israelites had a man who could defeat him, the greatest of warriors, the Philistines would become the Israelites' slaves. None of the frightened Israelite soldiers would rise to Goliath's challenge.

David, a young shepherd, was bringing food to his brothers, who were Israelite soldiers. Hearing Goliath's challenge, David told the Israelite leader Saul that he would fight Goliath. David believed that God would help him defeat the giant.

Armed with nothing but a rock and a sling, David faced the heavily armored Goliath. When the giant came toward him, David put the rock in his sling and slung it at Goliath, hitting him in the forehead. The giant fell to the ground. David then took Goliath's own sword and cut off his head.

When the Philistines saw that their leader was dead, they fled but were pursued and eventually defeated by the Israelites.

wise person is often said to have the "wisdom of Solomon," referring to the Old Testament king.

Many Bible stories have been retold in other forms. The popular musical play *Joseph and the Amazing Technicolor Dreamcoat* is based on the story of Joseph and his coat of many colors. John Steinbeck's novel *East of Eden* is a modern story based on the biblical story of Cain and Abel, the sons of Adam and Eve. Many younger readers know Isaac Bashevis Singer's book *Noah Chose the Dove*.

Bigfoot ❧ *See* FEARSOME CRITTERS.

Big Mosquitoes ❧ The subject of a TALL TALE from African American and other American folklore. Big mosquitoes have often been the subject of tall tales. In her book *Mules and Men*, for example, Zora Neale Hurston relates a story from African American folklore. In this tale, a man tells about his father, who waited out a rainstorm under a tree that was so big it would take six men to reach around it by holding hands. While he was leaning against the tree, a big mosquito made a hole right through the tree and bit the man on the other side.

One of the stories about Paul Bunyan (*see* PAUL BUNYAN AND BABE) tells of the "moskittos" in Bunyan's logging camp. They were so big "that they could straddle the stream and pick the passing lumberjacks off the log drive." Sometimes the loggers would tie the legs of one of these mosquitoes to trees and use the mosquito as a bridge over the river. Paul Bunyan tried to get rid of the mosquitoes by importing some fighting bumble bees from Texas. The bees and the mosquitoes fought for a while, but in time they made peace. The bees bred with the mosquitoes, and their offspring had stingers at both ends.

Billy the Kid's Adventures ❧

Tales told of an outlaw gunfighter who became a LEGEND in stories and

Billy the Kid in an etching from about 1880.

songs of the American Old West. Billy the Kid was born William Bonney in New York City, and the legends about him say that he killed his first man in a gunfight at age 12. He spent most of his brief career as a gunfighter in New Mexico. He served some time in a New Mexico jail, but he escaped by killing two guards. He boasted that he had killed a man for each year of his life.

Billy the Kid played a part in the range wars of the Southwest during the 1870s. Wealthy cattle owners John Chisum and Alex McSwain tried to take over the entire cattle-grazing business in the area. Their goal was to drive out all the other ranchers so that they could use all of the land for their huge herd of cattle. Many of the smaller ranchers banded together to fight Chisum and McSwain. Chisum hired Billy the Kid to help him fight the ranchers.

Billy the Kid was shot and killed on a moonlit night by Sheriff Pat Garrett, who had once been his friend. Garrett was with a party of law officers hunting down the Kid to stop him from stealing cattle.

Billy the Legend. Although the real William Bonney was a criminal, legend has made him into a folk hero (*see* HEROES OR HEROINES) of the American Southwest who could ride a horse better and shoot straighter than anybody. According to the leg-

end, he was kind to his mother and loyal to his friends. The cattle he stole were roaming freely on the range, and he never stole from innocent people. Like many such folk heroes, he was young, spirited, and energetic. He lived by his wits and courage in a wild, untamed region, and he died the way he had lived. [*See also* JESSE JAMES.]

Bluebeard's Adventures 🐚 A

FOLKTALE about an evil villain who marries women and then kills them.

Jennie Harbour, who illustrated this scene from "Bluebeard," worked in a style popular in the early twentieth century.

In the seventeenth century, the French writer Charles Perrault (*see* PERRAULT, CHARLES) published a collection of stories called *Tales of Mother Goose.* "Bluebeard" is one of the stories in that collection.

An Evil Villain. Bluebeard, named for the unusual color of his beard, is a villain. He is one of the most evil characters in the folklore of Europe, and his story is one of horror. In most versions, Bluebeard is either a nobleman or a wealthy merchant who hates women. He marries one woman after another and tells each wife that she must never open the door to a certain room in his castle. The women, who are usually sisters, either die or disappear because they open the forbidden door. In time, Bluebeard marries the youngest sister, who discovers the bodies of her murdered sisters in the secret room. She defeats Bluebeard either by her own cleverness or with the help of her brothers.

In the nineteenth century, the GRIMM BROTHERS included the story of Bluebeard ("Blaubart") in a famous story collection, *Nursery and Household Tales.* They included it because they wanted to show the devotion of the youngest sister and her brothers. The Grimm brothers, though, found the tale so horrible that they took it out and replaced it with another story in later versions of the collection.

The name Bluebeard survives today. Some people use it to refer to any man who is cruel, especially to women.

Boarhog for a Husband

An African American FOLKTALE about a man who changes into an animal. In African and AFRICAN AMERICAN FOLKLORE, many animals have human qualities or characteristics. In this story, told in the Bahamas and the southern United States, a king's daughter rejects one suitor after another. One day, however, a handsome young man arrives, and she falls in love. She tells her parents that this is the man she will marry. Her brother, Witch Boy, warns that the man is really a boarhog (a type of wild pig), but no one believes him. The story tells what happens when the princess and the young man marry.

The Story. After the couple married, the king gave them a plot of land on a mountaintop. The land was good for growing Tania, a favorite vegetable of both humans and boarhogs. Each day, as the husband went up the mountain to farm the land, he stopped at a little house along the way, where he would change into a boarhog. At noon, he would change back into a man before Witch Boy arrived with his lunch.

One day, Witch Boy arrived early and caught his sister's husband in the process of changing. He told his father, but the king did not believe him. When Witch Boy caught the boarhog a second time, the king decided to check for himself because, he said, a lot of Tanias were missing from his own fields. When the king witnessed the young man's transformation, he shot and killed him. The king and Witch Boy carried the carcass down the mountain. The daughter screamed when she saw her dead husband, but then she realized that her father had done the right thing.

Brer Rabbit and Tar Baby ❧

A story about a trickster (*see* TRICKSTERS) who first appeared in African folklore. Versions of this story can be found all over the world, including South America, Asia, and Europe, and among American Indians. The character Brer Rabbit is best known from an 1880 book of early African American stories collected by Joel Chandler Harris. The title of the book is *Uncle Remus: His Songs and Sayings.* Brer Rabbit is a sly rabbit who uses his wits to outsmart other animals, including Brer Fox and Brer Wolf. One of the most popular stories in the collection is about Brer Rabbit and Tar Baby.

The Story. Brer Fox wanted to catch Brer Rabbit, so he made a fake baby out of tar and put it in Brer Rabbit's path. Brer Rabbit hopped by and tried to talk to the tar baby but got no answer. In anger, he punched the tar baby. His arm stuck to the tar, so he struck again with his other fist, and then with his head and his feet. After Brer Rabbit became completely stuck to the tar baby, Brer Fox thought he could capture him. Brer Rabbit, though, tricked Brer Fox. He pretended to be scared and begged the fox not to throw him into a brier patch. Brer Fox, of course, then threw him right into the brier patch, where Brer Rabbit used the prickly briers to comb the tar out of his fur. He escaped, outwitting Brer Fox once again.

Bridger and the Obsidian Cliff ❧

A TALL TALE of the American Old West. Jim Bridger (1804–81) was a famous mountain man and fur trader of the American Old West. He was also an explorer who discovered amazing places and things. He was the first white man to see the area in Wyoming where Yellowstone National Park is now located. People thought Bridger was lying when he described some of his discoveries, such as the Yellowstone geysers—natural fountains of hot water that shoot high into the air from underground. Then Bridger actually did begin to tell fantastic tall tales about his travels.

The Obsidian Cliff. One of Bridger's more famous tales is about seeing the Obsidian Cliff in Yellowstone. The Obsidian Cliff is now a famous tourist attraction made of obsidian, which is a natural glass that is dark but transparent (you can see through it). Bridger's story of his experience with the cliff became his tale of the glass mountain. In that story, he claimed to have been hunting when he spotted a magnificent elk and fired at it. The elk was not wounded; it did not even seem to have heard the shot. Bridger fired at the elk three more times, but each time the same thing happened. Finally, he rushed toward the elk, planning to beat it to death with his rifle. But suddenly he crashed into a wall of transparent glass. The mountain of glass separated him from the elk. Even stranger, it acted like a telescope, so that, although the elk appeared to be only a few hundred yards away, it was really 25 miles off in the distance.

This carving of Buddha from a cave in central India was made 1,400 to 2,200 years ago.

Buddha and the Bodhi Tree ❧ A

MYTH, or sacred story, about Buddha, the main figure of the Buddhist religion. Buddha spent much of his life searching for enlightenment—an understanding of the meaning of life. He found it under the Bodhi tree. The Bodhi tree is a symbol that is similar to the cross in Christianity. The Bodhi tree stands for achieving a greater awareness of the universe by giving up everything in life except for the things one really needs, such as food, water, and basic clothing. Just as pieces of the cross are said to be kept in some Christian churches, pieces of the Bodhi tree are said to exist in some temples in Asia.

According to the story, Buddha sat under the Bodhi tree and refused to leave until he became enlightened. A demon called Mara realized that Buddha was about to receive enlightenment and tried to tempt him away from the Bodhi tree. Buddha was then tempted by three more demons, but he did not give in, and he became enlightened. People and even animals bowed down to show him respect. He remained under the Bodhi tree for seven days, then stood up for seven days to think about his new understanding of life.

Calamity Jane

Calamity Jane ❧ A woman of the American Old West, known for her shooting ability. Calamity Jane is the nickname of Martha Jane Burke, who was born Martha Jane Canary in 1852. She was an excellent shot with either a pistol or a rifle. Because of her shooting ability, she could "guarantee to bring calamity," or trouble, to anyone who made her angry. By the end of the nineteenth century, like Annie Oakley (*see* ANNIE OAKLEY AND HER GUN), she had become a LEGEND of the Old West.

The Real Calamity Jane. Calamity Jane was born in Princeton, Missouri. She moved to Virginia City, Montana, with her family when she was eight years old. Living in the Wild West, she believed that to survive she had to wear men's clothes and carry six-shooters. In time she became well known as a frontier scout, and she delivered mail for pony express companies. When South Dakota became a U.S. territory in 1861, she moved there. She traveled from one town to another before finally settling down. She died in 1903.

The Legend. Calamity Jane was a famous frontier character. She was known for being tough and hard-hearted, and many legends grew up

Calamity Jane holds the rifle she used to gain her reputation.

around her life. Some say she was a scout for George Armstrong Custer, an American general defeated by American Indians led by Chief Sitting Bull at the Battle of Little Bighorn. [*See* CUSTER'S LAST STAND— TWO VERSIONS.]

In the 1880s, author Edward Wheeler used Calamity Jane as a character in novels such as *Deadwood Dick on Deck* and *Calamity Jane, the Heroine of Whoop Up*. In the twentieth century, she was a character in western films. But these books and films probably do not present Calamity Jane the way she really was. Some people use the term *Calamity Jane* to refer to people who always have gloomy stories to tell or who always seem to bring trouble wherever they go.

Captain John Smith and Pocahontas

❧ The LEGEND, based on fact, of an Algonquin woman and a British captain. Captain John Smith (1580–1631) spent two years in America running Jamestown, England's first colony in the New World. At first, the Jamestown colonists and the local Algonquin tribe fought. During a battle, the Algonquins captured Smith and brought him before the tribe's chief, Powhatan. The tribe members were about to beat Smith to death with clubs when, according to Smith, Powhatan's 12-year-old daughter, Pocahontas, threw herself

The older Pocahontas in formal English attire.

over Smith's body to save him. According to legend, John Smith and Pocahontas were in love, but that is probably not true. Some people believe that the whole event was really part of a traditional American Indian adoption ceremony. In time, Powhatan adopted Smith as his son, and relations between the colony and the Algonquins improved. Pocahontas served as a messenger, bringing food, supplies, and news of her father's plans to the colonists.

After Smith returned to England, however, things changed. Pocahontas was captured and converted to Christianity. She later married a wealthy colonist, John Rolfe, and went to England with him. Pocahontas died in 1617 and is buried in England.

Chinook Ship Monster

A FOLKTALE of the Chinook people of Washington state. Many tales told by American Indians contain frightening monsters. One of the most terrifying is the windigo, a giant creature that sometimes eats its victims. There are also stories about an ogre who kicks people off cliffs and the tale of the IROQUOIS FLYING HEAD—a head with wings sprouting from its cheeks. In the tale of the Chinook ship monster, the terrifying creature comes from the sea.

The Story. A mother was grieving for her dead son when she looked out to sea and saw something that looked like a huge whale with spruce trees sprounting from its back. Then, creatures that looked like bears with human faces apeared on top of the monster whale.

The mother ran to her village in tears to warn the people about the monster. The villagers ran to the beach with their bows and arrows. When one of the men swam out and climbed on top of the whale, he found that it was on fire, so he swam back to shore.

The monster burned up. Only pieces of metal were left, which the Chinook sold. They became rich selling the parts of the monster that survived the fire.

An old sailing ship like the one that surprised the Chinook.

The Real Story. This story is based on fact. What the grieving mother really saw was a ship carrying Europeans to the shores of what is now Washington state. She had never seen a sailing ship with towering masts. To her it looked like a monster whale, and the masts looked like spruce trees. The sailors who appeared on deck looked like bears because of the long hair and beards, and the pieces of metal were parts of the ship, which was made mostly of wood. The wooden parts of the ship burned up in the fire.

Cinderella

Possibly the world's most famous and best-loved FAIRY TALE. People all over the world know the story of the girl who has to do all the work and live by the cinders, or ashes, of the fire, while her stepmother and stepsisters treat her badly. With the help of magic (*see* MAGIC OBJECTS AND WIZARDS), the girl goes to a ball, where a prince falls in love with her. After the girl leaves the ball, the prince searches for her. In the end, the girl proves who she is and marries the prince.

Hundreds of Cinderellas. Many different cultures tell the Cinderella story with different titles. For

"Aschenputtel": *A Grimm Brothers Story Similar to "Cinderella"*

The GRIMM BROTHERS of Germany also wrote a story about a hardworking girl who is rewarded for her goodness. But their story, called "Aschenputtel," is different from the Perrault story in some ways.

Aschenputtel, the heroine (*see* HEROES OR HEROINES), asked her father for a tree branch to plant on her mother's grave, which she visited three times a day. Whenever Aschenputtel made a wish at the grave, a white bird in the tree that had grown from the branch granted her wish (*see* HELPFUL ANIMALS).

When Aschenputtel's sisters were dressing for the ball, the stepmother (*see* WICKED STEPMOTHER) tossed a bowl of beans into the ashes and told Aschenputtel that she could go to the ball if she picked out all the beans. All the birds outside helped pick up the beans, but the stepmother did not keep her promise. It was the birds, rather than a fairy godmother, who gave the poor girl a magnificent dress and shoes so that she could go to the ball. But the story does not say how Aschenputtel got there. There is no magic coach, and there is no warning to return at midnight. Also, in "Aschenputtel," the prince himself arranged for the girl to lose her shoe so that he could later use it to find her.

Then the Grimm story gets gory. The stepsisters' feet were too big to fit into the shoe, so one girl cut off a toe and the other girl cut off part of her heel to make the shoe fit. The prince saw blood in the shoe and knew the sisters had cheated.

In the Grimm tale, as in Perrault, the prince finally finds his true love and marries her. The Grimm stepsisters, however, are punished for their cruelty. On the wedding day, the birds peck out their eyes. [*See also* YEH-SHEN.]

example, there are versions told by American Indians and versions from France, Germany, China (*see* YEH-SHEN), and Africa. The number of Cinderella stories is somewhere between 700 and 900. Most of them are similar, but each has its own details.

The French Version. In the United States, most children know the story written down by Charles Perrault (*see* PERRAULT, CHARLES) a Frenchman, about 300 years ago. This is the version that Walt Disney used when he made the animated cartoon about Cinderella in 1949.

In Perrault's version of the story, Cinderella dressed her wicked sisters for the ball, to which she could not go herself. When they left, Cinderella cried, and a fairy god-mother (*see* FAIRIES) appeared. With a wave of her magic wand, a golden coach, six horses, a jolly coachman, and six footmen appeared. With one more wave of the wand, the god-mother changed Cinderella's rags into a magnificent gown and a pair of glass slippers. As Cinderella left for the ball, the godmother warned her to be home by midnight.

At the ball, the prince danced with Cinderella and fell in love with her. But when the clock began to chime midnight, Cinderella dashed away, losing one of her glass slippers. The prince found the slipper and tried it on every girl in the kingdom to locate his true love. When it fit Cinderella, he married her. Cinderella, always kind to her mean stepsisters, brought them to live at the palace and found husbands for them. People who read this version of Cinderella know that everyone lives happily ever after.

This illustration of a fancy ball is by Arthur Rackham, a famous British artist.

Clemens, Samuel ❧ *See* TWAIN, MARK (1835–1910).

Clementine ❧ An American folk song about the California gold rush. Early in 1848, gold was discovered in California. This was the beginning of the California gold rush. In 1849, thousands of people went to California to seek their fortunes. They were called the "forty-niners" in reference to the year.

Many American folk songs were written about the gold rush and the forty-niners. "Clementine" is one of them. Although the story the song tells is sad, the words make it sound humorous. In one version, a miner grieves and pines away because his daughter has drowned. In another he kisses her little sister and forgets her. Here are the words to the former version:

> In a cavern, in a canyon,
> Excavating for a mine,
> Dwelt a miner, forty-niner,
> And his daughter, Clementine.
>
> *Chorus*
> Oh my darling, oh my darling,
> Oh my darling Clementine!
> Thou art lost and gone for-
>   ever,
> Dreadful sorry, Clementine!
>
> Light she was and like a fairy,
> And her shoes were number
>   nine,
> Herring boxes without
>   topses,
> Sandals were for Clementine.
>
> *Chorus*
> Drove she ducklings to the
>   water,
> Ev'ry morning just at nine,
> Hit her foot against a splinter,
> Fell into the foaming brine.
>
> *Chorus*
> Ruby lips above the water,
> Blowing bubbles soft and fine,
> But alas, I was no swimmer
> So I lost my Clementine.

Contest of Riddles ❧ An African tale that is really a RIDDLE. The tale describes what happened and then asks the reader to answer a question. Many African FOLKTALES follow this pattern. They are used to encourage people to discuss problems.

A king announced that his daughter was ready to marry, but she could marry only a man who could prove that he was wise in the knowledge of riddles. Many men tried and failed to win the king's daughter with their skill in riddles. Eventually, two men from a distant village decided to travel to the court to try their skill. Because they had a long way to travel, they hired another young man from their village to help them carry their things. To everyone's surprise, the young man was the one who solved the princess's riddle (*see* PRINCES OR PRINCESSES).

After the wedding, the suitors who had failed to win the princess demanded that the young man help them back to their village. On the way home, angry and jealous, they tied him to a tree and left him there to die. When a seller of kola nuts passed by, the young man asked him to take a message to the princess. The message was, "Untie this kola and guard it, or it will surely rot." The princess knew immediately that the message was from her husband and went to his rescue. At the end, the story asks the reader or listener to tell who knows more about riddles—the princess or her husband. [*See also* RIDDLES—A COLLECTION.]

Coyote, Iktomi, and the Rock ✢

A FABLE of the White River Sioux. In many stories about Coyote, he is a trickster (*see* TRICKSTERS). He makes listeners and readers laugh; he outwits even the rich and powerful. But in some tales, Coyote is punished for his outrageous behavior. That is the case in this story that also features the spider man, Iktomi, who is also a well-known trickster.

The Story. Coyote and Iktomi were walking along one day when they encountered a rock called Iya. In a moment of generosity, Coyote gave the blanket he was wearing to the rock. Then he and Iktomi continued walking.

Suddenly, it started to rain. The temperature dropped and the rain turned to slush. Shivering, Coyote wished he had his blanket, and he sent Iktomi to ask Iya to give it back. Iya refused, so Coyote himself went to ask for the blanket back. Again Iya refused, saying, "What is given is given." Coyote took the blanket anyway and joined Iktomi to wait out the storm.

When the sun came out again, the two friends heard a horrible rumbling noise. They looked up to find that Iya was rolling toward them very fast. They ran away, over rivers and through woods, but nothing, it seemed, could stop Iya. Iktomi turned himself into a spider and hid in a mouse hole. Eventually Iya caught Coyote and rolled over him, flattening him completely. Satisfied, he took back Coyote's blanket.

A person with an American Indian blanket like the one Coyote gave to Iya.

A rancher found Coyote's flattened body and decided he would make a nice rug. So he took him home and put him down in front of his fireplace. Although Coyote had the power to bring himself back to life, he was so flattened out by Iya that it took him all night to return to his usual shape.

The next morning, when the rancher asked his wife where his new rug was, she told him it ran away.

The Moral. A fable usually has a moral, and this one is no exception. "Always be generous in heart. If you have something to give, give it forever." [*See also* AMERICAN INDIAN FOLKLORE.]

Creation Myth ❧ *See* GREEK CREATION; SACRED STORY.

Cuchulain's Life ❧ A MYTH about an ancient Irish warrior. The story of Cuchulain (kü hül′in) is part of a group of Irish stories about the warriors who fought for the Irish ruler Conchobar (kon′ ä kär). Cuchulain was Conchobar's nephew and his greatest warrior.

The stories of Cuchulain describe his fearless, superhuman skills in battle. Brought up under his uncle's rule, Cuchulain was brave, loyal, and loved by women. One story tells that his father was a god and that Cuchulain's powers came from magical spells. When he was in combat, a "hero's light" shone from his forehead and blood spurted from his head. He was so fierce that he had to be cooled down after battle so he would not burn his fellow warriors. He died young, in battle, because he was tricked into eating the flesh of a dog, which would hurt his magical powers. Just before the battle, he ate the flesh with his left hand, and that hand lost all its strength. Cuchulain was speared, but he hauled himself up against a rock so that he would die standing up. The other warriors did not even know Cuchulain was dead until a raven landed on him. When he died, his sword fell and struck off his enemy's right hand.

Cupid and Psyche ❧ The Roman MYTH and FOLKTALE about the love between a beautiful woman and Cupid, the Roman god of love. In the romance between Cupid and Psyche, a beautiful mortal princess (*see* PRINCES OR PRINCESSES) is forbidden to know the true identity of her lover. The theme of a lover with a secret identity appears often in folklore.

The Story. Venus, the goddess of love, became jealous of the beautiful princess Psyche. Venus ordered her son, Cupid, to make Psyche fall in love with a monster by shooting her with one of his magic arrows. But the instant Cupid saw Psyche, he fell in love with her.

With the help of the god Apollo, Cupid made a plan to win Psyche for himself. Apollo ordered Psyche's father to leave his daughter at the top of a hill to wait for her husband—a terrible dragon. Psyche's unhappy father obeyed, thinking he was leaving his daughter to die. But on the hilltop, Psyche fell asleep and awoke near a magnificent palace. That night, Cupid came to Psyche. Psyche fell in love with her new husband, but she could not see him in the dark and did not know who he was. Cupid warned Psyche that she must never look at him. But one night the curious Psyche lit an oil lamp so that she could see her husband after he fell asleep. But a drop of oil from the lamp fell onto Cupid's shoulder and awoke him. He ran away because he was afraid that Psyche would tell her friends who he really was. Then Venus might find out that he had married Psyche instead of obeying his mother.

The unhappy Psyche, not knowing that Venus hated her, begged the goddess to help her find her husband. Venus promised to help Psyche but instead put her into a deep sleep.

Psyche would have slept forever if Cupid had not found her. He asked Jupiter, king of the gods, to protect them from Venus's anger. Jupiter changed Psyche into a goddess. Because not even Venus could oppose the marriage of a god and a goddess, the lovers were finally safe.

Custer's Last Stand—Two Versions

Two versions of the same LEGEND—one told by European Americans and one told by American Indians. Both are based on one historical event: the defeat of Lieutenant Colonel George Armstrong Custer and 260 of his soldiers at the Battle of Little Big Horn. This event has been considered a national tragedy, primarily by Americans of European descent. In one song from the 1930s, for example, Custer is described as "a hero of a hundred fights." But many Native Americans regard Custer as a villain, a coward, and a liar.

On June 25, 1876, Custer attacked a Sioux village near the Little Big Horn River in what is now Montana. In the battle that followed, Custer and all his soldiers were killed. Although many soldiers were scalped and mutilated, Custer's body was left untouched. Because it was common for warriors to take scalps, the fact that Custer was not scalped has suggested two different versions of the event.

The European American Version. For those who believe Custer is a hero, the fact that the Sioux left his body alone shows that the American Indians respected Custer's skill as a soldier. The American Indian version, however, is quite different.

The American Indian Version. Before the attack on the Sioux village, Custer had made a peace agreement

General Custer and the U.S. 7th Cavalry are surrounded by Sioux and Cheyenne Indians at the Battle of Little Big Horn.

with the Sioux. He had even smoked a pipe with the tribal council. When he left the council, Black Kettle, a peace chief, said that if Custer broke his promise of peace, he would die a coward's death, and no warrior would dirty his hands by taking his scalp.

Custer did break his promise, which is why he was not scalped. The American Indian version of the legend adds that Custer had a woman's knife in his body when he was found. This was a way of saying that he was so cowardly he could be killed by a woman.

A Victory and a Defeat. Although the Battle of Little Big Horn was a victory for American Indians, it caused the U.S. government to increase its efforts to drive the Indians out of Montana and the Dakotas. In the end, the battle led to defeat for the Sioux and several other tribes. [*See also* HEROES OR HEROINES.]

Daniel Boone's Exploits ❧ Some

legends about the American frontiersman. In the years since his death in 1820, stories about Daniel Boone have been told many times by many different people. These storytellers have often used Boone's real-life exploits, along with exaggeration and fictional tales, to create a hero of the frontier and to portray Boone as the ideal American. Although he was not formally educated, the storytellers have said, he was wise in the ways of the forest and of American Indians. They claimed that he brought civilization to the wilderness, but that he

Daniel Boone and the Spirit of the Forest

This is a tale about the American woodsman and hunter Daniel Boone. Boone was hunting bear one evening in the deep, dark forest when he heard a voice. As he peered through the undergrowth, he saw a pair of huge green eyes staring back at him. Boone had heard American Indian tales about spirits who live in forests and streams. Now he began to wonder. Maybe he had been unable to find any bears that day because an evil spirit had chased them all away. Maybe the spirit was after him too. Boone moved toward the eyes he had seen with his rifle aimed and ready. Suddenly he heard a voice asking him not to shoot—*please.*

Boone lowered his gun. Out from the bushes stepped a young girl with shining green eyes. She told him that she had gotten lost in the woods while picking berries. Boone offered to walk her home. He took her by the hand to lead her safely through the woods. Boone did not shoot any bear that day, but he fell in love with the green-eyed girl, who later became his wife.

himself preferred to be independent of others, away from towns and cities. They praised Boone both as a fierce fighter and as a defender of peace.

Boone the Tracker. Two stories are told about Daniel Boone's tracking ability. The first concerns his daughter and her friend, who, it is said, were captured and taken hostage by a party of American Indians. When Boone realized the girls were missing, he tracked them through the forest, even though the Indians did everything they could to cover their tracks. When Boone caught up with them, he howled like a forest spirit and attacked, even though he was alone.

The Indians were so sure that Boone could not have tracked them, they decided he must have flown over the treetops with the help of forest spirits. When the captors ran away in terror, Boone was able to rescue the girls.

In another story, Boone was himself held captive by a band of American Indians. When Boone's captors heard a shot near the camp, they went to investigate, and Boone managed to escape. But first, he carved three large notches in an ash tree.

Nearly 30 years after this incident, Boone was asked to help settle an argument about a piece of land. A man said that one corner of his property was marked by the same ash tree Boone had carved years before. Boone said he thought he could find the tree, even though he had moved away from the area and the land had undergone many changes since he had been there.

Boone led the man to an ash tree, which appeared to have no notches. Boone then used his axe to cut away the bark on one side of the tree, and when he did, there were the three notches. The property owner was suprised at Boone's ability to find this particular tree with so little to guide him. [*See also* HEROES OR HEROINES; LEGEND.]

David and Goliath ✎ *See* BIBLE STORIES.

Davy Crockett and the Alamo ✎

A LEGEND based on a historical event. Many stories have been told about Davy Crockett, an American frontiersman and a member of Congress from Tenessee. The theme song from the 1950s Disney television series based on Crockett's life, for example, claims that Davy "kilt him a b'ar [bear] when he was only three" and "patched up the crack in the Liberty Bell."

Remember the Alamo! Although Davy Crockett is remembered for many exploits—some true, some exaggerated, and some purely fictional—he is perhaps best remembered as one of the heroes of the

Alamo. It was at the Alamo, an old mission converted into a fortress, that Texans and Hispanic Texans known as *tejanos* (ta‾ háhn o‾s) fought for the independence of Texas from Mexico. The Texans were eventually defeated and most were killed, but their bravery inspired others to fight for and finally win independence. Their battle cry was "Remember the Alamo!"

Davy Crockett and the others who fought at the Alamo knew that they were fighting against great odds. There were fewer than 200 men inside the fort, whereas the Mexican general, Santa Anna, had a huge army on his side.

According to the legend, Davy Crockett was the bravest of the brave. In the fighting, he seemed to be "everywhere at once—shooting at Mexicans, handing bullets to his friends, shoving an enemy through a window, shouting praise to the Indian warrior who had come to help the Texans."

Crockett's body was never identified, and there were several stories telling how he died.

The truth was not known until 1975, when the diary of a Mexican soldier was published. Lieutenant José Enrique de la Peña revealed that Crockett and several others were taken prisoner. They were

Davy Crockett holds his rifle above his head.

brought before Santa Anna, who ordered them bayoneted and shot. Peña said that Crockett and the others died bravely. [*See also* TALL TALE.]

Deep Snow ❦ An American TALL TALE that describes the weather in comic and exaggerated terms. American folklore is full of stories, sayings, and superstitions about the weather. Tales such as this one celebrate the American land and people by portraying the weather as bigger and more violent in America, and especially in the American West, than anywhere else in the world.

In this particular tale, a man rode his horse to the courthouse in a snowstorm. When he arrived in town, the courthouse was closed. He tied his horse to what he believed was a hitching post, spread a blanket on the snow-covered ground, and went to sleep. When he awakened the next morning, the snow had melted. He searched for his horse, only to find that what he thought was a hitching post was actually a church steeple. The snow had completely covered the church so that only the steeple was sticking up! The man drew his pistol, shot off the reins to free his horse, and rode away.

Devils ❦ *See* JONATHAN MOULTON AND THE DEVIL; MOMOTARO'S STORY.

Dragons ❦ *See* FEARSOME CRITTERS; HELPFUL ANIMALS.

Dwarfs ❦ *See* FAIRIES; RUMPEL-STILTSKIN.

Eena, Meena ❦ The first words in the most widely known GAME RHYME in the United States. "Eena, meena, miny, mo," is the beginning to a popular four-line counting rhyme that children use to decide who is "it" or to choose sides for a game. Often the words *eena meena* are pronounced *eeny meeny*.

Although the first line of the rhyme appears to be nonsensical, it can actually be traced back many hundreds of years to the Druids, priests who lived in ancient Ireland and Wales and who used a similar rhyming chant, "eena meena, mona, mite," to select victims for human sacrifice.

Baron Munchhausen's "Snow Storm"

Similar to DEEP SNOW, "Snow Storm" is a TALL TALE told in the eighteenth century by Baron Münchhausen, a German officer in the Russian army. His tall tales were gathered in a collection known as *The Adventures of Baron Münchhausen*.

In the 1850s, children in the United States heard a French Canadian version of the rhyme. They translated the French in the second line into English words that sounded similar to the French. Thus, the French word *cache*—meaning, "hide"—became *catch*, and *dos*—"back"—became *toes*. The original French line was "Hide your fist behind your back." Today the rhyme is said like this:

> Eeny, meeny, miny mo,
> Catch a tiger by the toe.
> If he hollers, let him go.
> Eeny, meeny, miny mo.

El Dorado ❧ After Spanish explorers discovered the Americas, a LEGEND spread of a vast store of gold in the New World. Many explorers came from Europe to search for El Dorado (which means *the gold*) throughout Central and South America. In the ancient stories, El Dorado was an American Indian chief who was covered in gold dust and threw gold and jewels into a lake as a sacrifice. Later, El Dorado referred to a mythical place where the chief's gold was supposed to be located. In England, the explorer Sir Walter Raleigh published a book about his search for the mythical El Dorado, popularizing the story in Europe. Now *El Dorado* is used to describe an impossible goal.

Elves ❧ *See* FAIRIES; SANTA CLAUS.

Elvis, the Once and Future King

❧ Elvis Presley, a rock star of the 1950s, 1960s, and 1970s, about whom legends (*see* LEGEND) have arisen. Although he died in 1977, many of Elvis Presley's fans refuse to believe that he is actually dead, and they claim to have seen him in various places. These claims are called *Elvis sightings*. The belief that he still lives on links Elvis, who was nicknamed "the king," with KING ARTHUR. Although Arthur was killed in a battle, stories about him said that he was not really dead and would reappear when Britain got in trouble. For this reason, King Arthur came to be called *the once and future king*. Because of the belief that he has appeared after his death, Elvis Presley has also been called *the once and future king*.

European American Folklore ❧

The folklore of Americans of European descent. To many people, the word *folklore* immediately brings to mind peasants, kings, dragons, FAIRIES, and the idea of "once upon a time, long ago." These people are thinking about the folklore of Europeans, Asians, Africans, or American Indians. European American folklore goes back only a few hundred years and tends to be about pioneers, lumberjacks, clever Yankees, and cowboys. One can often trace a FOLKTALE back to the real-life person or event on which it was based. Davy Crockett (*see* DAVY CROCKETT AND THE ALAMO), for example, was a real person, even if he didn't kill a bear before his third birthday. Although a European folktale about a princess might have been based on a real princess (*see* PRINCES OR PRINCESSES), the origin of the story is likely to have been lost.

Folklore American Style. European American folklore was influenced by European tales, but it soon developed its own themes, characters, and style. One typically American feature is the habit of exaggerating. For example, in many tales, characters boast about their own abilities, the awfulness of the weather, or the impressiveness of the landscape (*see* BRIDGER AND THE OBSIDIAN CLIFF; DEEP SNOW; TALL TALE). American folklore suggests that American mountains are always the highest, American rivers always the widest, and American characters always the best—or the worst.

Another important difference between European American folklore and older folklore has to do with the relative youth of American culture. The first European folktales, for example, were oral and probably went through many versions before they were written down, but many American folk sayings, stories, and anecdotes were preserved in writing from the beginning.

Folklore often takes place in exotic or impressive settings.

The heroes (*see* HEROES OR HEROINES) of American folktales tend to be one of two major types. One is the clever Yankee; the YANKEE PEDLAR is a good example of this type. The other is the western hero, which includes frontier settlers such as Daniel Boone (*see* DANIEL BOONE'S EXPLOITS), railroad workers such as JOHN HENRY, and loggers such as Paul Bunyan (see PAUL BUNYAN AND BABE).

The Yankee is hard-working, sensible, thrifty, and hard to fool. The western hero is strong, courageous, and often larger than life. [*See also* AFRICAN AMERICAN FOLKLORE; AMERICAN INDIAN FOLKLORE; FOLKTALES; TALL TALE.]

Fable ❧

A tale with a moral. The purpose of a fable is to teach people how they should behave in order to live good lives. Some fables make fun of how foolish people behave rather than teach a lesson. Many fables involve animals who talk and act like people.

In general, a fable has two parts. The first part tells a story. The second part contains the moral—advice to the reader or listener, often stated in the form of a PROVERB. For example, in AESOP's fable "The Ant and the Grasshopper," the grasshopper plays

A *Fable:* "Nasreddin and the Donkey"

This Turkish FABLE teaches people to think for themselves instead of being influenced by the opinion of others.

One day Hodja Nasreddin and his son went on a journey. Hodja did not want to ride their donkey, so he told his son to ride. As they went along, they passed some people who said, "Look at that boy riding the donkey. He is young and healthy, so he must not have any respect for his father if he rides and makes his father walk."

The boy felt embarrassed and told his father that he did not want to ride the donkey. Hodja mounted the donkey and his son walked. Soon they passed some other people who said, "Look at that selfish man. He rides while his little son must walk."

Now Hodja felt ashamed and climbed down from the donkey. "Maybe the best thing would be for both of us to walk," he said to his son.

The father and his son continued on, both walking, holding the donkey by his halter. Soon they passed some people who said, "Look at those foolish people. Even though they have a donkey, both of them are walking."

When the people had passed, Hodja said to his son, "See how hard it is to escape from the opinions of others."

all summer long while the ant works. When winter comes, the ant has enough food, but the grasshopper is starving. The moral is, "It is best to prepare for the days of necessity."

A fable differs from a FOLKTALE in that it is a story deliberately crafted by a writer for the purpose of teaching a lesson, as opposed to a story told or written merely for entertainment.

[*See also* BRER RABBIT AND TAR BABY; COYOTE, IKTOMI, AND THE ROCK; JACOBS, JOSEPH; NEVER HOLD YOUR HEAD TOO HIGH; OLD MAN COYOTE AND THE BUFFALO; PANCHATANTRA; PARABLE; THE POOR MAN AND THE SNAKE; PUSS IN BOOTS; THE TORTOISE AND THE HARE.]

Fairies ❧ Fictional characters who have magical powers. Fairies have supernatural powers, meaning they can do things that human beings and animals cannot. For example, fairies can live forever and can change form

---

A Celtic Fairy Tale: "Soul Cages"

Like his father and grandfather, Jack Dogherty was a fisherman. He wanted very much to see a merrow, one of the sea people. His grandfather had had a friendship with one a long time ago.

One stormy day in a cave, Jack finally met a merrow with green teeth, a red nose, pig's eyes, a fish's tail, legs with scales, and short arms like fins. His name was Coomara, and he invited Jack to put on a magic hat and go with him to his house beneath the sea. There they had dinner and much brandy, a strong drink.

Later, Coomara showed Jack his lobster pots, which he called *soul cages*, because they held the souls, or spirits, of sailors drowned at sea. Back on land, Jack worried about the souls trapped in those pots. So he came up with a plan.

Jack invited Coomara to his house and served him an even stronger drink called *poteen*. It put Coomara to sleep. Then Jack grabbed the magic hat, went down into the sea, and opened all the soul cages to set the souls free. Feeling better, Jack arrived back at his house just in time to find Coomara waking up. Coomara put on the hat and went home. They say that Coomara never knew who freed the souls. They also say that Coomara never drank poteen again.

Tiny fairies often live in unusual places, such as inside a flower.

Fairy Godmother ❧ *See* FAIRIES.

Fairy Tale ❧ Originally, a kind of FOLKTALE that involves FAIRIES. But now the term *fairy tale* can mean a story that deals with magic and fantasy but that does not have to include fairies. Most fairy tales, including "Hansel and Gretel," contain at least some of the following features:

- a battle between good and evil
- a reward for the good and punishment for the evil
- a happy ending

or make themselves invisible. Most of the time, fairies are tiny. Sometimes they play tricks on humans (*see* TRICKSTERS) or bring harm to them. At other times, fairies show favor to humans and help them.

One particular kind of fairy is the fairy godmother, who can help HEROES OR HEROINES of a story. A fairy godmother plays a large role in the story CINDERELLA.

Fairies also have other names: brownies, dwarfs, elves, gnomes, goblins (*see* GHOSTS AND GOBLINS), leprechauns, and pixies. (In A Celtic Fairy Tale: "Soul Cages" the fairy creature is called a *merrow*. The Celts lived in Ireland and other places a long time ago.)

An illustration of "Hansel and Gretel" by Arthur Rackham.

- a scary setting such as a dark forest
- a danger such as a poison
- characters such as animals that can talk, dwarfs, giants, PRINCES OR PRINCESSES, step-parents, fairies, WITCHES, GHOSTS AND GOBLINS, or other supernatural beings

Many fairy tales that started out as oral, or spoken, stories a long time ago were later written down by collectors such as Charles Perrault, (see PERRAULT, CHARLES) of France, the GRIMM BROTHERS of Germany, and Andrew Lang (see LANG, ANDREW) of Scotland. Other fairy tales originated as written, not oral, stories.

Many famous written fairy tales were created by Hans Christian Andersen (see ANDERSEN, HANS CHRISTIAN) of Denmark and Rudyard Kipling (see KIPLING, RUDYARD) of England.

A Fairy Tale: "Hansel and Gretel"

Hansel and Gretel were the children of poor parents. When food ran out, the mother decided that she and her husband should take the children deep into the woods the next day and leave them there alone. Without the children, she said, the two adults would have enough food to live. The children heard the plan, so the next day, Hansel left a trail of pebbles behind him as the family walked into the woods. Later, Hansel led Gretel back to the family's house by following the trail.

The mother did not give up. She insisted on taking the children deeper into the woods and abandoning them there. This time Hansel used breadcrumbs to leave a trail, but birds ate the crumbs. The children were near starvation when they came upon a gingerbread house—a house they could eat! But soon Hansel and Gretel realized that the house was a trap. They were the prisoners of a wicked old witch (see WITCHES), who wanted to eat them.

The children knew they had to kill the witch in order to save themselves. They tricked her into bending over to look into the hot oven—and then Gretel pushed her in. Before the children ran off, they found many pearls and precious stones, which they took. When Hansel and Gretel arrived home, their father, who had never wanted to hurt them, was joyous. And the evil mother, the children learned, had died.

Some people use the label *fairy tale* for any fantastic story, such as *The Wonderful Wizard of Oz* and *Peter Pan*. [*See also* BEAUTY AND THE BEAST; CINDERELLA; FASTING FOR THE HAND OF THE QUEEN'S DAUGHTER; THE FISHERMAN AND HIS WIFE; JACK AND THE BEANSTALK; THE KING'S DAUGHTER WHO LOST HER HAIR; MOTHER HOLLE; THE NIGHTINGALE; THE ROOSTER, THE MOCKINGBIRD AND THE MAIDEN; RUMPELSTILTSKIN; THE TALKING EGGS.]

Fasting for the Hand of the Queen's Daughter

A FAIRY TALE from the Bahamas, in which a pigeon and an owl, who used to be friends, compete for a woman whom each wants to marry. Contests—especially contests in which the prize is marrying a powerful person's daughter—are very common in folklore. Sometimes the stronger competitor wins; sometimes the more clever competitor wins.

In this tale, the pigeon and the owl competed to see who could last longer without eating. The winner would marry the queen's daughter. The pigeon did not play by the rules, though: he ate berries and drank dew when no one could see him. In the end, the pigeon won the contest. The story gives readers and listeners a lot to think about. For example, they might wonder, "Why does the animal that cheats win? Shouldn't the more honest animal win? Is cheating ever all right?"

Fearsome Critters

A general name for monsters and other scary living things talked about by people on the American frontier in years past. (*Fearsome* means "frightening." *Critters* is one way people say the word *creatures*.)

Americans did not invent the first monsters. Scary creatures probably started with nightmares that ancient people had. In sculptures,

Bigfoot

All over the world, especially where there are forests, people have reported seeing a gigantic, hairy creature that walks standing up on two legs. No one has ever captured one or provided absolute proof that it exists. To this day, people argue about the monster: Is it real?

The creature has different names in different parts of the world. In Mongolia, it is called the *almas*. In China, its name means *the wildman*. In the Himalayan mountains, it is known as *Yeti* or *the Abominable Snowman*, and in the northwest part of North America, it is called *Sasquatch* or *Bigfoot*.

paintings, and stories from all over the world, monsters loom. Sphinxes (*see* OEDIPUS AND THE RIDDLE OF THE SPHINX) and centaurs look partly human; gargoyles, unicorns, and dragons are entirely nonhuman but may combine the real and the make-believe.

Even though Americans were not the first to invent monsters, they did create the monsters known as *fearsome critters*. Some Americans believed they really saw monsters.

American Indian Stories. Some American Indian myths (*see* MYTH) tell about good monsters, but most tell about scary ones. In the tradition of the Hopi people, ogres called *soo'so'yoktu* arrive in February and frighten children, while grownups think about things they have done wrong. Finally, the people force the ogres from the village and celebrate.

European American Stories. Europeans who came to America brought tales of monsters. They changed the monsters and created strange new ones to better fit the American landscape. For example, they made up the black hodag, a swamp beast that eats human flesh, and the hoop snake, which puts its tail in its mouth and rapidly rolls over the woodland like a hoop.

African American Stories. Stories handed down by African slaves often involve TRICKSTERS. A trickster is often a character with the strength of an animal and the tricky mind of a human (*see* COYOTE, IKTOMI, AND THE ROCK). Other stories deal with beasts disguised as humans, as when a beautiful woman marries a handsome man only to find out he is really a boarhog (*see* BOARHOG FOR A HUSBAND).

Asian American Stories. The most common make-believe Asian animal to come to America is the dragon. In the rest of the world, a dragon is usually fearsome, but in Asian and Asian American cultures, the dragon is usually a kind beast (*see* HELPFUL ANIMALS).

Febold Feboldson ❧ A Swedish character who appears in many American tall tales (*see* TALL TALE) told by another character—his great nephew Bergstrom Stromberg. The nephew describes the uncle as "the most inventingest man." Story after story tells about an invention or idea of Febold's. Some of his inventions caused problems of their own.

One story, for example, reported that Febold had the idea to carry California desert sand in wagons across the snowfields of Nebraska. His goal was to melt the snows. He accomplished his goal, but as a result of Febold's plan, the prairies of Nebraska are incredibly hot in summertime.

Another story told how Febold put dogs on a treadmill. He had noticed that dogs turn around three times before lying down. When they did their turning on a treadmill, they started a windmill, which then pumped water for Febold's livestock.

Yet another story claims that Febold even invented certain animals. Febold, the story goes, figured out how to save chickens by making them into a new animal, which the Indians called *ducks*.

Finn Mac Cool

A legendary Irish hero (*see* HEROES OR HEROINES; LEGEND). Finn Mac Cool (whose name is sometimes given as Fionn MacCumaill or Mac Cumhail) was the chieftain, or leader, of a band of warriors who were also poets. The group's name was the Fenians, or the Fianna. Supposedly, they lived in the second or third century C.E. According to the legend, Finn was a relative of a druid, or priest or wizard, and he was raised in a forest.

The Fisherman and His Wife

A tale by the GRIMM BROTHERS, showing what can happen when people become greedy and selfish.

A poor fisherman caught and then threw back a fish that was really an enchanted prince. The fisherman's wife demanded that her husband call back the fish to grant a wish for a cottage to replace their poor hut. The wife got her wish but was not satisfied. Four more times

A scene from "The Fisherman and His Wife" by John Gruelle (1880–1938).

the fish fulfilled her wishes. The cottage became a castle, and the wife became king, emperor, and pope. All along, the sea got stormier. Then the wife went too far. She wished to be God, and the couple found themselves back in the hut forever. [*See also* THE POOR MAN AND THE SNAKE.]

Folk Song

See BALLAD AND FOLK SONG.

"Bear Man Tale": *A Cherokee Folktale*

Here is a shortened version of the story: a hunter tried to kill a bear with his bow and arrow but failed. The man thought, "This must be a medicine bear, a being that has special powers." Indeed, the bear, who could read minds, then invited the hunter to share his shelter and food during the winter. After they stopped at a meeting of other bears, the medicine bear and the hunter went into the bear's home. There, two amazing things happened. First, the bear got berries and nuts simply by rubbing his stomach. Second, the hunter's hair grew, and the hunter began acting like a bear.

When spring came, the bear told his guest what would happen in the future. He said that other hunters would kill the bear and rescue the hunter. He gave instructions to the hunter: "Cover my blood with leaves, and as you go off with the other men, look back at the leaves." What did the man see when he looked back at the leaves? He saw the bear rise up out of the leaves and walk calmly into the woods.

Perhaps ancient people used this story to explain the mystery of hibernation.

Folktale ❧ A story that has traveled across generations, usually at first by word of mouth rather than in writing. By now, most of the world's folktales have been written down.

Every culture, or group of people, has folktales, which describe the people—their strengths and weaknesses, joys and sorrows, and nightmares and dreams. The writer Virginia Hamilton says, "Folktales are our self-portraits."

Even when different groups tell different stories, there are ideas that are the same from folktale to folktale. For example, most folktales contain characters or events that do not appear in the everyday world. Most folktales also involve magic and sometimes a magical change (*see* MAGIC OBJECTS AND WIZARDS). Finally, in most folktales, wicked people are punished, and the good are rewarded.

The FAIRY TALE, the TALL TALE, and the FABLE are three special kinds of folktales. [*See also* ALI BABA AND THE FORTY THIEVES; BABA YAGA TALE; THE BAKER'S DOZEN; BEAUTY AND THE BEAST; BLUEBEARD'S ADVENTURES; BOARHOG FOR A HUSBAND; BRER RABBIT AND TAR BABY; CHINOOK SHIP MONSTER; CUCHULAIN'S LIFE; CUPID AND PSYCHE; IROQUOIS FLYING HEAD; JONATHAN MOULTON AND THE DEVIL; LITTLE RED RIDING HOOD; MARWE IN THE UNDERWORLD; MOMOTARO'S STORY; OEDIPUS AND THE RIDDLE OF THE SPHINX; PUSS IN BOOTS;

THE QUEST FOR THE GOLDEN FLEECE; THE QUEST FOR THE HOLY GRAIL; SLEEPING BEAUTY; SUPERMAN; TILL EULENSPIEGEL AND THE BEEHIVE; YANKEE PEDLAR.]

Frankie and Johnny ❧ An American LEGEND about the romance between a woman named Frankie and a man named Johnny. This lesson is told in a ballad (see BALLAD AND FOLK SONG). American folklore is full of songs about the great joy and great pain that love brings. Such songs tell what happens when two people are in love and one person hurts the other.

People who study folklore say that even though we do not know who wrote "Frankie and Johnny," the ballad probably has African American roots. They also say that the story is similar to events that happened to real people in the 1800s in North Carolina and in St. Louis, Missouri.

The Story Line. "Frankie and Johnny" has 27 stanzas. The first stanza sets the stage.

> Frankie and Johnny were
>   lovers, oh Lordy, how
>   they could love,
> Swore to be true to each
>   other, just as true as
>   the stars above.
> He was her man, but he
>   done her wrong.

The last line of the stanza tells that Johnny did something wrong and hurt Frankie's feelings. Finally, to-ward the end, the line is spoken by Frankie and changes in an important way:

> "He was my man, and I
>   done him wrong."

The details are as follows: Johnny went out with another woman. In some versions, Johnny and Frankie had already broken up when he went out with Alice Pry. Even so, Frankie had given her money to Johnny, so she was not happy that Johnny was spending it on someone else. Frankie plans her revenge on Johnny.

Game Rhyme ❧ A song that children sing as they play certain games. (The games are usually not electronic and do not require cards, boards, or playing pieces.)

Two of the most popular game rhymes are the circle song (see HERE WE GO ROUND) and the jump rope rhyme. In a jump rope rhyme, as soon as the rope skipper misses, she or he is out, and someone else gets a turn to skip. Some jump rope rhymes tell funny stories; some make fun of people; and, depending on when the skipper misses, some jump rope rhymes are said to predict the skipper's future or tell a secret.

In hide-and-seek, "it" uses a rhyme to warn the hiders that the search is about to begin and another rhyme to make the children come out of hiding. [See also EENA, MEENA;

Jump Rope Rhymes

Here are some rhymes heard 30 years ago at Peabody Elementary School in Washington, D.C., and on many other playgrounds too. They are similar to rhymes from all over the world and still heard in the United States.

Grandma, grandma, sick in bed,
Called for the doctor, and the
      doctor said,
"Grandma, Grandma, you ain't
      sick,
All you have to do is the seaside
      six."
Hands up, shakey, shakey,
      shakey, shake,
Hands down, shakey, shakey,
      shakey, shake,
Touch the ground, shakey,
      shakey, shakey, shake,
Get out of town, shakey, shakey,
      shakey, shake.

MATTHEW, MARK, LUKE, AND JOHN; RIDE A COCKHORSE; TEASING RHYME.]

Genies ❧ *See* MAGIC OBJECTS AND WIZARDS.

George Washington and the Cherry Tree ❧ *See* LEGEND.

Ghosts and Goblins ❧ Two kinds of imaginary, supernatural characters. Ghosts and goblins are supposed to do things that human beings and animals cannot. They seem to appear at night, many times in wrecked buildings and in lonely graveyards, but some people tell stories about seeing ghosts during the daytime.

In some stories, ghosts and goblins act friendly. In others, they cause only small damage, such as breaking dishes, or they may do evil deeds, such as kidnapping children.

Some people believe that ghosts are the spirits of dead people who make trouble for the living because they are jealous of them.

Goblins are considered a type of fairy (*see* FAIRIES). In stories, goblins look strange or ugly. They live in

It is very common for people to be afraid of ghosts and goblins, especially of ghosts. People may even wear charms to keep ghosts away.

Halloween

GHOSTS AND GOBLINS have major parts on Halloween, a holiday that falls on the last day of October. Far back in history, before the time of Christ, there was a festival of the dead on a certain night. People thought that on this night, ghosts came back to the homes they lived in when the ghosts were alive. They also thought that WITCHES and other demons, or evil spirits, wandered through the world on this night.

When the Christian religion came about, this holiday was selected as the time to remember the dead, including saints (called *hallows*) and *martyrs* (people killed for their beliefs). It became "All Hallows' E'en" (Eve) or "Halloween" and was celebrated on the evening before All Hallows', or All Saints', Day.

People who celebrate Halloween perform many rituals, or customs and ceremonies. In addition to carving jack-o-lanterns, people dress up as ghosts, goblins, witches, and other characters and go from house to house. They are called trick-or-treaters and demand sweets for *not* making trouble. Large outdoor fires called *bonfires* are set because of the old belief that they will keep away evil spirits.

dark places, and they are also strong, cunning, or sly. Some people use the term *hobgoblin* to mean "any goblin," but other people use *hobgoblin* only for goblins that are not evil. [*See also* THE SICK MAN'S GHOST.]

Giants ❧ *See* FAIRY TALE; FEARSOME CRITTERS; JACK AND THE BEANSTALK; JACK TALES

Glooscap Slays the Monster ❧

A TALL TALE with amazing descriptions and a MYTH that explains where bullfrogs come from. The story belongs to the Algonquin tribes of the northeastern part of the United States.

Glooscap is many things to the Algonquin Indians. He is part man and part god. As a creator, he made his people and their original villages and animals; he also makes and changes other living things. As a hero (*see* HEROES OR HEROINES), he protects his people. As a trickster (*see* TRICKSTERS), he can change his shape and appearance. In this story, Glooscap appears as all three—creator, hero, and trickster.

The Story. Glooscap heard that his people were in trouble because the spring had no more water. One man reported that up north a gigantic water monster had stopped the water from flowing down to the Algonquin people. This disgusting monster would not consider helping

A bullfrog like the one the monster Glooscap fought.

the people. The only thing he would think about was eating them.

Glooscap prepared to fight the water monster by making himself enormous and making a sharp knife out of a mountain of flint, which is a hard, gray stone. When Glooscap and the monster met, Glooscap showed he was not afraid. He called the monster insulting names and then sliced its stomach open, letting out a roaring river, which would always keep the Algonquin alive. As a finishing touch, the enormous Glooscap squeezed the gigantic monster until it became a bullfrog. To this day, bullfrogs make a croaking sound like the sound the water monster made, and they have wrinkled skin because Glooscap squeezed the monster so hard. [*See also* FEARSOME CRITTERS.]

Gnomes ❧ *See* FAIRIES.

Goblins ❧ *See* GHOSTS AND GOBLINS.

Gods and Goddesses ❧ *See* GREEK CREATION; HOW CORN CAME; SPIDER GRANDMOTER LEADS THE PEOPLE.

The Good Samaritan ❧ A PARABLE, or brief story that teaches a lesson, found in the New Testament of the Bible. In ancient times, the Samaritans were people who lived in Samaria, a part of Palestine. Jews and Samaritans were not friendly toward each other. However, in the parable told by Jesus, a Samaritan stops to care for a Jewish traveler who has fallen ill. The Samaritan helps the Jew, even though two religious Jews have already passed by without helping. The message of the parable is that everyone should show kindness, mercy, and love to anyone who is unfortunate.

Greek Creation ❧ The story of how the world began, told by the people who lived almost three thousand years ago in the land now known as Greece.

The ancient Greeks believed that Earth was the first living thing and that Earth made Sky. Earth and Sky had many children who themselves had many children— powerful beings called gods and goddesses. At times, they would

A sculpture of the Greek god Zeus.

FABLE, JOKE, or another form of folklore that already existed. Today, the Grimms are best remembered for the fairy tales, especially such famous ones as CINDERELLA, "Snow White and the Seven Dwarfs," and LITTLE RED RIDING HOOD.

The Grimms tried to make the stories they wrote better than the ones they heard spoken. They also tried to make the language smoother and more colorful, the plots easier to understand, and the events more suitable for young children. [*See also* THE FISHERMAN AND HIS WIFE; MOTHER HOLLE; OUR LADY'S LITTLE GLASS; SLEEPING BEAUTY.]

fight. The most powerful god was Zeus. The gods and goddesses lived forever. Humans were also created, but they could not live forever. Sometimes they mated with gods and goddesses and produced mighty children, called heroes. [*See also* HEROS OR HEROINES; OEDIPUS AND THE RIDDLE OF THE SPHINX; THESEUS GOES TO HIS FATHER; TROJAN HORSE.]

Grimm Brothers ❧ Two German brothers who collected and published old stories, most of which had never before been written down. Almost every story that Jacob (1785–1863) and Wilhelm (1786–1859) wrote was a FAIRY TALE, LEGEND,

The Grimm Brothers as they looked about 1830.

Halloween *See* GHOSTS AND GOBLINS.

Hansel and Gretel *See* FAIRY TALE.

Helpful Animals ❧ In a MYTH, FABLE, FAIRY TALE, or FOLKTALE, animals that can often speak or understand human beings and that can help HEROES OR HEROINES. Sometimes helpful animals appear in modern literature too, such as the spider in *Charlotte's Web* and the lion in *The Chronicles of Narnia*. Every culture, or group of people, has stories that tell about helpful animals.

Some helpful animals do only small chores. For example, in the Disney version of "Snow White and the Seven Dwarfs," the birds help Snow White clean up the cottage. Usually, though, helpful animals deal with matters of life and death. The bear in "Bear Man Tale" (*see* FOLKTALE) gives the hunter food and shelter all winter. At other times, a helpful animal might say, "Enough is enough." An example is the fish (really an enchanted prince) in THE FISHERMAN AND HIS WIFE.

Hanuman, the Helpful Monkey

For about two thousand years, people in India and other countries have been reciting or reading the very long Hindu poem called *Ramayana*. The poem tells the story of Prince Rama, who was part god and part human. Monkeys helped Rama at an important point in his life.

Rama had married Sita, who possessed some powers of a goddess. Then a band of monkeys saw the evil king of the forest kidnap Sita from Rama. One monkey named Hanuman promised to find Sita and bring her back. First Hanuman found Sita on an island. Then the monkeys built a bridge to the island. Rama and his forces crossed the bridge and killed the evil king. Sita was returned to Rama.

People who study folklore have noticed something special in stories that tell about helpful animals: The human characters in these stories *must* listen to the animals in the same way that humans should always listen to their own instincts, or feelings.

Here We Go Round

Here We Go Round ❧ A song sung as children join hands and move, or dance, around in a circle (*see* GAME RHYME). All cultures, or groups of people, have circle songs and games. "Here We Go Round" uses a lot of repetition. Here is part of the song.

> Here we go round the
> mulberry bush, the
> mulberry bush, the
> mulberry bush;

Walter Crane (1845–1915), an Englishman, did this charming illustration of children singing "Here We Go Round."

> Here we go round the
> mulberry bush,
> All on a frosty morning.
>
> This is the way we clap our
> hands,
> This is the way we clap our
> hands,
> This is the way we clap our
> hands,
> All on a frosty morning.

Heroes or Heroines ❧ In stories, characters who solve conflicts, or problems, even at the cost of their lives. Most stories—those that end happily and those that end sadly—have one or more heroes or heroines.

Sometimes the hero or heroine is an ordinary person. For example, in "Hansel and Gretel" (*see* FAIRY TALE), an ordinary girl acts heroically when she kills the wicked witch (*see* WITCHES). However, in most stories that have lasted for hundreds or thousands of years, the hero or heroine is more than ordinary; he or she shows extraordinary courage, strength, intelligence, or kindness. For instance, heroes include the brave character in "David and Goliath" (*see* BIBLE STORIES), the strong character in GLOOSCAP SLAYS THE MONSTER, the intelligent character in OEDIPUS AND THE RIDDLE OF THE SPHINX, and the kind character in BEAUTY AND THE BEAST. [*See also* QUEST FOR THE GOLDEN FLEECE; QUEST FOR THE HOLY GRAIL; TRICKSTERS.]

How Antelope Carrier Saved the Thunderbirds and Became Chief of the Winged Creatures ❧ A

story about a poor boy who achieved greatness. In many American Indian folktales (*see* FOLKTALE), animals talk and think like people. The Arikara Indian story of Antelope Carrier is one of these.

A Poor Boy . . . A Great Hunter. Once there was a boy whose parents were very poor. Because the wood rats pitied him, they made him a bow and some magic arrows. The arrows helped the boy shoot as many antelopes as his family needed to eat. His skill earned the boy the name Antelope Carrier.

The Thunderbirds. Antelope Carrier set off to explore the world. He made camp by a large lake and fell asleep by the campfire. When he woke, he found himself on top of a mountain with a nest of four baby Thunderbirds—supernatural creatures who brought the thunder.

Soon the mother Thunderbird appeared and told him that she and her husband had never been able to raise any young because a two-headed monster in the lake rose up and devoured the babies before they could leave the nest.

Antelope Carrier agreed to help. Soon the monster appeared. The Thunderbirds created a huge storm and hurled lightning bolts to try to protect their young, but their weapons were useless against the monster. Antelope Carrier took a magic arrow from his quiver, strung his bow, and shot the arrow into the monster's open mouth. When the arrow entered the monster's mouth, it became a tree, causing the monster's head to explode. Then Antelope Carrier shot another magic arrow, which hit the monster's neck and cut off his other head.

The Thunderbirds were grateful to Antelope Carrier and made him king of all winged creatures.

How Corn Came ❧ An American

Indian MYTH about where corn comes from. Different groups of American Indians have different versions of the story, but all tell of a god or goddess who dies and then gives the gift of food to the people.

From the Ojibway Indians. A young man named Wunzh went to a far-off place alone. He wanted to get more food for his people, and he hoped that by fasting, or not eating, the gods would reward him. Wunzh was weak from not eating, when he saw a person in yellow and green come down from the sky. The person said he would help Wunzh, explaining, "Tomorrow your father will bring food. Eat it. You will wrestle with me several times and win. Then take my clothes, bury me, and keep weeds away from that spot."

All these things happened. Later, Wunzh found a tall plant of yellow corn with a green husk on the spot. His friend had come back. Wunzh told his people how to care for the corn so that they would always have food.

From the Penobscot Indians. After a man and First Mother had children, and the children had children, there were not enough animals to feed everyone. First Mother said her husband must kill her and her sons must pull her by her silky hair over the earth until her flesh scraped off. Sadly, they did what she asked.

Seven months later, the children returned to find sweet and tender

A design using ears of corn, an important food for American Indians.

corn, which came from their mother's flesh. They ate some and saved some for the future.

How the Leopard Got His Spots
🐾 *See* KIPLING, RUDYARD.

Ibbity, Bibbity 🐾 A GAME RHYME for counting out. Some counting-out rhymes are used to pick the person who will be "it" for a game such as hide-and-seek. Other counting-out rhymes are used to eliminate players until only one person remains—the winner. Whoever the leader is pointing to when he or she gets to the end of the rhyme is "it" or is out.

Here is one version of "Ibbity, Bibbity."

> Ibbity, bibbity, sibbity, sab,
> Ibbity, bibbity, canal boat,
> Canal boat in, canal boat out,
> Canal boat over the water spout
> O–U–T spells out!

Line 3 might mean "Canal boat into a lock, canal boat out of a lock." (The lock is where a boat is raised or lowered in the water so that it will be able to sail into the next part of a canal.) Line 4 might be about the rush of water that comes out of a lock. [*See also* MATTHEW, MARK, LUKE, AND JOHN.]

Iroquois Flying Head 🐾 A scary story in which a young Iroquois woman goes up against an awful monster. This monster is only a head,

An Iroquois warrier: The Iroquois told the story of the flying head.

but a head with wings coming out of its cheeks. The head is also as tall as four men, and its mouth has teeth that tear apart living things. The head's favorite meal is human beings.

One stormy night, the head came out of his home to find someone to eat among the Iroquois people. All the people in the tribe's house ran out—all except one young woman with a baby. When the head looked into the house to find something to eat, he saw her by the fire. It looked like she was eating the burning rocks and enjoying them. So the head helped himself to the heap of hot stones. Of course, he screamed and flew away. According to the story, no one knows what happened to the flying, burning head.

This story shows an ordinary person becoming a heroine (*see* HEROES OR HEROINES). By acting bravely and using her brain, the young woman defeats the enemy. [*See also* FEARSOME CRITTERS.]

Irving, Washington (1783–1859)

An American author who is known for the LITERARY FOLKTALE, which is based on German stories but given an American setting. For example, the setting of "Rip Van Winkle" and "The Legend of Sleepy Hollow"—the two most famous of Irving's stories—is the Hudson River

A portrait of the author Washington Irving, about 1830.

Valley and Catskill Mountains of New York state. "Rip Van Winkle" tells about a man who fell asleep for 20 years. "The Legend of Sleepy Hollow" concerns the fears of a school teacher traveling home at night.

Today, readers note that Irving's stories have hard words, long sentences, and expressions that sound strange to them. Still, readers continue to read them for the spooky details and humorous characters.

from "The Legend of Sleepy Hollow" *by Washington Irving*

Here are a couple of paragraphs from the story.

All the stories of ghosts and goblins that Ichabod Crane had heard in the afternoon now came crowding upon his recollection. The night grew darker and darker; the stars seemed to sink deeper in the sky, and driving clouds occasionally hid them from his sight. He had never felt so lonely and dismal. He was, moreover, approaching the very place where many of the scenes of the ghost stories had been laid. In the center of the road stood an enormous tulip tree, which towered like a giant above all the other trees of the neighborhood, and formed a kind of landmark. Its limbs were vast, gnarled, and fantastic, twisting down almost to the earth, and rising again into the air. . . .

As Ichabod approached this fearful tree, he began to whistle; he thought his whistle was answered: it was but a blast sweeping sharply through the dry branches. As he approached a little nearer, he thought he saw something white, hanging in the midst of the tree: he paused and ceased whistling; but on looking more narrowly, perceived that it was a place where the tree had been scathed by lightning, and the white wood laid bare. Suddenly he heard a groan—his teeth chattered and his knees smote against the saddle: it was but the rubbing of one huge bough upon another, as they were swayed about by the breeze. He passed the tree in safety, but new perils lay before him.

Jack and the Beanstalk

Jack and the Beanstalk ❧ An English FOLKTALE from Britain and the United States. People in other countries, such as Russia, tell stories similar to "Jack and the Beanstalk," but each version is a little different.

The Story. Jack and his mother were poor. One day, Jack's mother told him to take their cow to town to sell her and to bring back the money. But foolish Jack sold the cow for colored beans instead of money. When he got home, his mother was upset and threw the beans out the window.

By the next morning, an enormous beanstalk had grown. Jack climbed up it to the sky, where he found a giant's castle. When Jack entered the castle, the giant said the following rhyme:

> Fee–fi–fo–fum
> I smell the blood of an
> Englishman.
> Be he live or be he dead,
> I'll grind his bones to
> make my bread.

Hidden from the giant by the giant's wife, Jack watched the giant's

red hen lay a golden egg. Later, Jack stole the hen and brought it home. The next day, he climbed up again and stole the giant's gold. The third day, he stole the giant's golden harp,

The giant chased Jack down the beanstalk in this classic tale.

"Jack and the King's Girl"

Jack liked to visit his uncle. On his way to and from his uncle's house, he would pass the king's house and see the king's daughter. She had never laughed. The king had announced that the person who made the princess laugh could marry her.

When Jack was on his way to his uncle's house, the girl always told him to have a good time. When Jack was on his way back home to his mother's house, he always had a gift from his uncle, but the girl always called Jack a fool for the way he was bringing the gift home. Jack always explained he would follow her advice the next time. The problem was that the advice would not make sense "the next time."

One time Jack was walking home with a little horse that his uncle had given him. The girl said, "You ought to *ride* that." Jack answered, "Well, I'll try to think of that next time." The next time, Jack was bringing home a little cow. Remembering what the princess had said about the horse, Jack tried to jump on the cow's back. He fell off and grabbed on to the cow's tail. Then the cow started jumping and dragging Jack. Jack bounced along and hollered. When the princess saw Jack in this situation, she laughed. The king saw that his daughter was laughing, and he laughed also. Someone finally caught the cow and helped Jack. Then the king took Jack and his daughter to a church to get married.

but the harp cried out, and the giant chased Jack down the beanstalk. Jack slid down to Earth and chopped down the beanstalk, killing the giant. After that, Jack and his mother were no longer poor.

A Closer Look at the Folktale. This story has features that appear in other folktales as well. For example, many folktales tell of a fool who sells something in a ridiculous way. Also, magic objects (such as the beans, the red hen, and the talking harp) and ogres (such as the giant) often appear in folktales. Stealing and murder, too, are common themes. [*See also* MAGIC OBJECTS AND WIZARDS; JACK TALES.]

Jack Tales ❧ A group of stories about the hero (*see* HEROES OR HEROINES) in JACK AND THE BEANSTALK and "Jack the Giant-Killer." These stories are told in Britain, in the United States (originally in North Carolina and Tennessee), and in Europe, where sometimes the hero's name is Juan, Jean, or Hans.

Jack's personality is what ties all the stories together. Jack is, above all, too lazy to work, so he depends on luck or uses his brain to figure out how he can make money. Often, he takes on the task of stealing from giants and killing them.

Jacobs, Joseph (1854–1916) ❧

A British historian who gave much of his time to listening to and collecting folklore, especially the form known as the FABLE. Jacobs showed that a FOLKTALE could travel from one country or culture to another. For example, he pointed out how stories from India were similar to stories from England. [*See also* GRIMM BROTHERS; PERRAULT, CHARLES.]

Jesse James (1847–1882) ❧ One

of the most famous and feared gunfighting out-laws who lived in the Wild West during and after the Civil War.

Jesse Woodson James was born in Missouri in 1847. By the time he was 15, he had joined a gang of raiders who supported the South. After the Civil War, he started his own gang with his brother, Frank, and with three brothers—Cole, James, and Robert Younger. In spite

The outlaw Jesse James about 1870.

of the fact that he robbed banks and railroad trains and killed people during the robberies, James was considered a hero (*see* HEROES OR HEROINES) by some—perhaps by people who thought he was brave to live the lonely life of a gunfighter.

In 1882, back in Missouri, James was killed by Robert Ford, a member of his own gang. Ford apparently wanted to collect the $10,000 reward that the governor of Missouri had promised for turning in Jesse James—dead or alive.

Reality or Fiction? There is no doubt that Jesse James and his gang really existed. But James became a LEGEND, too, and a legend goes *be-*

yond historical facts to make a person larger than life. According to one of the legends, for example, James was like ROBIN HOOD, who stole from the rich to give to the poor. In real life, however, there is no proof that James was generous in that way.

Some of the reports about James that have come down through the years are based on actual events. For instance, the details of the 1876 raid on a bank in Northfield, Minnesota, are accurate. The robbery was a failure, and everyone in the gang except Jesse and Frank was caught or killed. However, a story that claims James showed up another gunslinger, "Wild Bill" Hickock, during a shooting match is pure fiction.

Joe Magarac ❧
A fictional American character whose family was said to come from Hungary. After Joe Magarac appeared in written stories, he became a folklore hero (*see* HEROES OR HEROINES). In other words, Magarac moved from the written page into spoken stories instead of the other way around.

Magarac is described as an extremely strong man like the folklore heroes Paul Bunyan (*see* PAUL BUNYAN AND BABE) and JOHN HENRY. He has been called a man of steel because he was born in a mountain of iron. He was so strong that he could squeeze melted metal with his bare hands to make rails for trains to run on!

Joe Magarac was said to have squeezed metal with his bare hands to make rails for trains to run on, as the men are doing here.

The most sensational story about Magarac tells how he melted down his own body of steel to use in building a new steel mill. [*See also* TALL TALE.]

John Darling's Lies ❧
Examples of the kind of American folklore called a TALL TALE, which is an exaggeration, or stretching, of the truth. John Darling tales are about life in the countryside. Topics include working on a barn, swimming in a pond, and getting and eating pancake syrup from maple trees. The tales are told in the voice of John Darling himself.

Each one of these stories starts out sounding ordinary but ends with a boast by Darling that is so extreme, so ridiculous, that the reader or listener knows Darling is making it up.

For example, in one story, Darling begins by saying he went for a swim and found an underwater Indian graveyard. That much of the story is believable. However, Darling goes on to say that he "stayed down an hour, walking up and down, reading the names and inscriptions on all them stones." That last comment turns the story into an exaggeration, or tall tale. Usually, the comment makes the reader or listener laugh at its silliness.

In all of Darling's tall tales, Darling talks in a dialect. Instead of saying *chimney*, he pronounces the word *chimley*. Instead of saying, "right here at home," he says, "right here to home." Finally, Darling often uses the words *ain't* and *'taint*.

John Henry   ❧ A hero (*see* HEROES OR HEROINES) who is a "natural-born steel-drivin' man."

Background. The story of John Henry has become a TALL TALE, but parts of it probably did happen during the laying of railroad tracks in West Virginia in the 1870s. At the time, strong men pounded long steel rods into rock to make deep holes. Then workers put explosives into the holes and exploded rock to make train tunnels. A worker called a *shaker* held the steel steady as another man used a 12-pound hammer to pound the steel into the rock.

In the late 1800s, all sorts of machines were being invented. Many of these machines left men without jobs. One machine was the steam drill, which was used in place of a man with a hammer.

John Henry Beats the Steam Drill. In a race with a steam-driven drill, John Henry used two 20-pound hammers—one in each hand. He hammered steadily for many hours. Finally, he began to tire, but he still did more work than the machine—before he collapsed and died.

As time passed, people added details to the story, and different versions developed. For example, some people say that at birth John Henry weighed 33 pounds; others say 44. In most versions, John Henry is African American; in one, he is white. Sometimes the story is simply spoken. Often, though, the story is sung as a ballad (*see* BALLAD AND FOLK SONG; JOHN HENRY'S HAMMER). But regardless of the details, John Henry is a folk hero because he represents the victory of the human being over the machine. Perhaps, in the computer age, the legend of John Henry is more meaningful than ever.

John Henry's Hammer   ❧ An American ballad (*see* BALLAD AND FOLK SONG). Most versions of the ballad use the dialect, or variety of language, of some southerners. Here

are the beginning lines as written down by John and Alan Lomax.

> John Henry was a li'l baby,
>   uh-huh,
> Sittin' on his mama's knee,
>   oh, yeah,
> Said: "De Big Bend Tunnel
>   on de C.&O. road
> Gonna cause de death of me,
> Lawd, Lawd, gonna cause
>   de death of me."

. . . .

> Cap'n says to John Henry,
> "Gonna bring me a steam
>   drill 'round,
> Gonna take dat steam drill
>   out on de job,
> Gonna whop dat steel on
>   down,
> Lawd, Lawd, gonna whop
>   dat steel on down."

> "John Henry tol' his cap'n,
> Lightnin' was in his eye:
> "Cap'n, bet yo' las' red cent
>   on me,
> For' I'll beat it to de bot-
>   tom or I'll die,
> Lawd, Lawd, I'll beat it to
>   de bottom or I'll die."

Here are lines from the middle of the ballad.

> John Henry tol' his shaker,
> "Shaker, you better pray,
> For, if I miss dis six-foot
>   steel,
> Tomorrow'll be yo' buryin'
>   day,
> Lawd, Lawd, tomorrow'll
>   be yo' buryin' day."

> John Henry tol' his captain,
> "Looka yonder what I see—
> Yo' drill's done broke an'
>   yo' hole's done choke,
> An' you cain' drive steel
>   like me,
> Lawd, Lawd, an' you cain'
>   drive steel like me."

Here are lines from the end of the ballad.

> John Henry was hammerin'
>   on de mountain,
> An' his hammer was strikin'
>   fire,
> He drove so hard till he broke
>   his pore heart,
> An' he lied down his hammer
>   an' he died,
> Lawd, Lawd, he lied down his
>   hammer an' he died.

[*See also* JOHN HENRY.]

Johnny Appleseed ❧ The nickname for John Chapman (1774–1845), who devoted his life to planting apple orchards on the American frontier. As one generation after another heard the story of his life, Chapman became a hero (*see* HEROES OR HEROINES) of folklore.

Originally from Massachusetts, Chapman spent 12 years in the area around Pittsburgh, Pennsylvania, caring for an orchard he had planted. Then he decided to take loads of appleseeds farther west, to Ohio and Indiana, so that the pioneers would have apple orchards also. He collected seeds from mills where apple cider was made and traveled by horse, canoe, and foot so that he could plant his seeds in remote, or far-off, places.

According to LEGEND, Chapman became homeless and dressed strangely. One report says

Generally, even in the coldest weather, he went barefooted, but sometimes, for his long journeys, he would make himself a rude pair of sandals; at other times he would wear any cast-off foot-covering he chanced to find—a boot on one foot and an old brogan [work shoe] or moccasin on the other. . . . His dress was generally composed of cast-off clothing, that he had taken in payment for apple trees. . . . In his later years, . . . his principal garment was made of a coffee sack, in which he cut holes for his head and arms to pass through.

In spite of his strange appearance, Chapman was said to be treated with respect by both Indians and by European settlers.

More Than the Apple Trees. Besides bringing the apple trees to the frontier, Johnny Appleseed was said to have a second goal: bringing religion to people in the wilderness. It is said that when settlers gave him

A U.S. postage stamp showing John Chapman (Johnny Appleseed) in front of a large red apple.

a place to sleep, he would open his worn-out Bible to the New Testament and read to them.

During the War of 1812, Johnny supposedly took on the job of warning settlers of trouble. Whenever he learned that the Indians fighting for the British were planning an attack, he would run through the woods to sound the alarm.

Johnson, James Weldon (1897–1938) ❧ African American novelist, poet, teacher, supporter of civil rights, and collector of African American literature and folklore.

One of his novels, published in 1912, is *The Autobiography of an Ex-Colored Man*. It tells the story of a black man who chooses to pass himself off as a white man. Even more important than Johnson's poetry, fiction, and essays is his work collecting and publishing the poems, spirituals (religious folksongs), and folktales created or passed down by other African Americans (*see* BALLAD AND FOLK SONG; FOLKTALE). By writing down these pieces of literature, which up until then existed only as spoken words, Johnson helped save important parts of African American and American history.

Joke ❧ A story, usually brief, with a funny conclusion. Much of the time, a joke travels by word of mouth rather than in written form, but in the age of the Internet, many jokes rapidly spread around the globe.

"The Creation" *by James Weldon Johnson*

James Weldon Johnson was a highly educated person, and all of his poems are considered very high quality. The word *literary* describes them. Sometimes Johnson used elegant, formal, even old-fashioned English, as in "Lift Ev'ry Voice and Sing," which is known as the Negro National Anthem. Here are the final two lines from that poem:

> Shadowed beneath Thy hand,
> may we forever stand,
> True to our God, true to our native land.

James Weldon Johnson would often write as if he were an African American minister enthusiastically preaching a sermon in the language of ordinary people. One example of such a poem by Johnson is called "The Creation." In this poem, Johnson tells in his own words the story of the creation of the world as explained in the Bible. He begins by giving God the following lines:

> I'm lonely—
> I'll make me a world.

Then Johnson writes about God's creation of night and day, the heavens and Earth, the animals, and, finally, human beings.

He includes images that would be familiar to his people. For example, he says that the Great God was "like a mammy bending over her baby." [*See also* GREEK CREATION; LITERARY FOLKTALE.]

Jokes fall into several categories. One category is wordplay—such as KNOCK, KNOCK jokes or puns, in which one word or sound has two meanings. An example of a pun is, "He works as a baker because he kneads (needs) the dough" (*dough* can also mean "money"). Another kind of joke is designed to mock, or make fun of, someone, as when a stand-up comedian imitates a politician. [*See also* RIDDLE.]

Jonathan Moulton and the Devil

❧ An early American FOLKTALE that tells the story of a man who makes a deal with the devil.

The main character in the story "Jonathan Moulton and the Devil" is very rich, but he is not satisfied. Moulton wants to be richer. He wishes he could be the richest man in the world. Then the devil appears. The devil offers to make Moulton's wish come true on one condition. Moulton must agree that when he dies, the devil will take Moulton's soul. In other words, the devil will make Moulton rich, but when Moulton dies, he will go to hell, not to heaven. Moulton agrees to this condition.

The rest of the story tells how Jonathan Moulton tries to outsmart the devil. He tries to get more money from the devil than the devil has agreed to give. In the end, though, Moulton is the one who is outsmarted.

Bargaining with the Devil. The story "Jonathan Moulton and the Devil" probably grew out of similar stories told by Europeans who settled in America. These European stories go back to the LEGEND of Dr. Johann Faust (1480–1540). Like other folktales, "Jonathan Moulton" and its older versions were first passed around by word of mouth instead of in writing. Later on, they were written down, and some versions have become very famous. For example, Washington Irving (*see*

The devil sometimes gives people what they ask for.

IRVING, WASHINGTON) wrote a story called "The Devil and Tom Walker." Stephen Vincent Benét wrote a version called "The Devil and Daniel Webster." In all these stories, a character is willing to give up a happy life after death for riches during his or her lifetime. When a character makes such a bargain with the devil, it is often said that the character "sold his or her soul to the devil."

The Juniper Tree ✸ A FAIRY TALE

by the GRIMM BROTHERS about how a boy suffers because of his stepmother and how he gets revenge (*see* WICKED STEPMOTHER).

The tale began by a juniper tree—an evergreen with berries—where a woman was praying for a child. When the berries ripened, she ate them. Finally, she had a baby boy, but she died, and her husband buried her under the juniper.

After the boy's father's new wife had a baby girl, the wife was mean to the boy. Once she invited him to pick an apple from a chest. Then she slammed the lid, cutting off the boy's head. Frightened, she put the head on the body and tied a kerchief around the boy's neck. Later, she told her daughter to slap the boy. His head rolled off. Blaming the girl for his death, the mother said they must hide the truth, so she chopped up the boy, made stew out of him, and fed the stew to her husband!

The girl put the bones from the stew below the juniper. Fire came out of the tree, and then a beautiful bird appeared, which flew to a goldsmith's shop. It sang that its mother had killed it and its father had eaten

"My Mother Killed Me": *Like* "The Juniper Tree"

African Americans tell a story very much like THE JUNIPER TREE, in which the cruel parent is the boy's own mother, not a stepmother. The tale does not say why the mother killed the boy, but as in "The Juniper Tree," the woman served the boy as a meat dish to the boy's father. Also as in "The Juniper Tree," the boy's sister took the bones left over after the father ate and put them below a tree—an almond tree rather than a juniper.

The boy's spirit then turned into a bird, which flew around singing a sad but beautiful song about his family—his mother the murderer, his father the innocent diner, and his sister Marjileta. When goldsmiths heard the song, they gave the bird presents of gold. The bird gave one of the gifts to Marjileta and used the other gift, a heavy stone of gold, to kill the mother.

A scene from "The Juniper Tree" by John Gruelle (1880–1938).

it. The goldsmith gave the bird a chain. The bird flew to a shoemaker's shop, sang its song, and got shoes. Finally, at a mill, the bird got the heavy stone that ground the grain to make flour.

The bird gave the father the chain and the girl the shoes as gifts. When the stepmother went outside, the bird dropped the millstone on her and killed her. A burst of fire flared up and then cleared. Standing in place of the bird was the little boy.

Just So Stories ❧ Twelve stories created by the English writer Rudyard Kipling (*see* KIPLING, RUDYARD) for his own children and then, in 1902, published as a book. Each story explains how something in nature came about. For example, the stories include "How the Elephant Got His Trunk," "How the Leopard Got His Spots," and "How the Camel Got His Hump." Although these stories were created and written down by Kipling, they are very similar in style to folklore stories that pass through a culture by word of mouth and change each time.

An illustration by Rudyard Kipling for "The Cat That Walked by Himself" from *Just So Stories.*

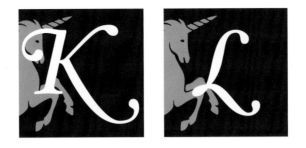

King Arthur

King Arthur ❧ The hero (*see* HE-ROES OR HEROINES) of a LEGEND based on a sixth-century Celtic warrior. (The Celts lived in Britain a long time ago.) The earliest stories about Arthur have him performing great deeds and displaying superhuman powers. A few hundred years later, stories have knights and ladies surrounding Arthur. All the knights are chivalrous, or very kind and helpful, toward the ladies. Stories of love between Arthur's brave knights and beautiful ladies became popular.

In the fifteenth century, a knight named Thomas Malory created a great English version of the King Arthur legend. It is called *Le Morte d'Arthur*, or *The Death of Arthur*. In this telling, Arthur is extremely moral, or good and honest.

Stories about Arthur did not end with Malory, however. Novelists, dramatists, and moviemakers have worked and played with the legend of the hero known as Arthur.

The Sword in the Stone. As in much other folklore, one story about Arthur concerns a magic object (*see* MAGIC OBJECTS AND WIZARDS). The story tells that a beautiful sword had been thrust into a block of marble. Holding the sword in place was a tool called an anvil. On the anvil were golden letters that read, "Whoever pulls out this sword from this stone and anvil is by right of birth king of all Britain." Arthur, and only Arthur, was able to remove the sword from

A scene showing King Arthur at the end of his life.

the stone. When Arthur was later crowned first knight of the realm, he swore to rule justly.

The King's Daughter Who Lost Her Hair

An African FOLKTALE about the virtue of generosity.

A wealthy king's daughter had a beautiful face and the most glorious long hair. The princess bragged about her riches but would not share them with a bird that visited her and complimented her. So the bird put a curse on the princess, and soon the curse came to pass: the princess lost all her hair!

A very poor and lonely young man named Muoma hoped to win gold promised by the king and set out on a long journey to find new hair for the princess. He too was visited by a bird, and when asked to give the bird some of his beans, he did so. He even gave a bean to a flower that requested it. After these two generous acts, Muoma received the secret for finding new hair for the princess. The king rewarded Muoma by giving him the gold as well as his daughter's hand in marriage.

This kind of African folktale is called a wonder tale. The story involves magic, and in that way it is like many folktales and fairy tales (*see* FAIRY TALE) from Europe or the Americas. The African tale is also similar to western tales in another way: the bad person is punished and taught a lesson, whereas the good person receives a reward.

Kipling, Rudyard (1865–1936)

A British author who is well known for novels, poetry, and children's stories. He was especially good at making a children's story sound like a FABLE or a FOLKTALE.

Kipling was born in Bombay, India, and loved the country. Much of his writing shows respect for the details of Indian life as he saw it. Even so, some readers criticize Kipling for believing, like many others in the nineteenth century, that the British had the right to rule over India and other distant parts of the world.

Rudyard Kipling in the early 1900s.

"How the Leopard Got His Spots" *by Rudyard Kipling*

Here is a brief version of one of the pieces by Rudyard Kipling in his JUST SO STORIES. The story begins by saying that long ago the leopards in the southern grasslands of Africa were a "yellowish-grayish-brownish color." Because leopards blended into the land so well, they could sneak up on the other animals. Eventually, these animals went to the forest and changed their skins so that they blended into it.

One day a leopard asked the baboon where the other animals had gone. "The game," said the baboon, "has gone into other spots; and my advice to you, Leopard, is to go into other spots as soon as you can."

So the leopard and his friend the Ethiopian hunter went into the forest, where they could hear and smell the giraffes and zebras but could not see them, for those animals had grown blotchy and stripy and blended into their background. Once the leopard and the Ethiopian hunter had figured this out, the Ethiopian told the leopard he should take the baboon's advice and "go into spots." The Ethiopian thought the advice meant that the leopard should *put spots on his skin*. So the leopard agreed. The Ethiopian put spots on the leopard, and ever since, all the leopards have had their spots.

Kipling's collections of stories for children include *The Jungle Book* and the JUST SO STORIES. The second title contains stories that explain how something in nature came about or why something is "just so." [*See also* LITERARY FOLKTALE.]

Knock, Knock ✌ A type of RIDDLE or JOKE that has existed in the United States since 1930. A knock, knock follows a routine exchange between two people. The person who begins the joke ends up putting words together in unexpected ways, surprising the other person. Here are a few examples from Duncan Emrich, who collected many knock, knocks.

First person: Knock, knock
Second person: Who's there?
First person: Amos.
Second person: Amos who?
First person: A mosquito bit me.

First person: Knock, knock.
Second person: Who's there?
First person: Andy.
Second person: Andy who?
First person: And he bit me
    again.

Krsna Steals the Clothes ✹ A

Hindu tale in which Krsna, a human form taken by the god Visnu, steals the clothes of the milkmaids as they bathe naked in a river. In this story, Krsna (sometimes spelled *Krisna* and *Krishna*) seemed at first to be acting like a trickster (*see* TRICKSTERS) for he told the girls to come out of the water and show him their naked bodies if they wanted to get back their clothes. Then Krsna explained that he was giving the girls a chance to bow low and ask forgiveness for swimming naked in front of another god, the god of the waters. In this way, Krsna helped the girls.

The religion of Hinduism is practiced mainly in India. It has three chief gods who represent the force from which all life flows. The gods may appear on Earth in various human forms. Hindus have created many stories involving the gods and human beings. In small villages in India, storytellers called *pandits* still recite the stories from memory, but by now the stories have been written down.

A sculpture of the Hindu god Shiva performing the dance of creation.

Lang, Andrew (1844–1912) ✹ A

Scottish collector of folklore as well as a historian, poet, author, translator, and editor. Lang was one of the first to realize that anthropologists, who study beliefs and life, must learn about each MYTH, FOLKTALE, and FAIRY TALE told by the people they are studying. Lang became well known for the 12 volumes in which he retold fairy tales. Each volume had a color in its title. For example, they are called *The Blue Fairy Book*, *The Red Fairy Book*, *The Lilac Fairy Book*, and so on.

Legba Steals God's Yams ✹ A

tale told by the Fon people of Benin in West Africa. Legba, like other

TRICKSTERS, has a good side and a bad side. In the beginning, he takes orders from his father, God. If things go well, the people give God the credit; if things go badly, the people blame Legba.

When Legba gets tired of this arrangement, he tells God that thieves are planning to steal yams from God's garden. In response, God tells his men that the thieves must be killed. Then Legba steals God's sandals and leaves God's footprints in the garden while taking the yams. Of course, the people then accuse God of stealing from himself. The result is that God leaves Earth and goes to live in the sky. Legba then becomes a messenger to God, reporting every night on the people of Earth.

Legend ❧ A story handed down, perhaps originally in speech rather than in writing, concerning historical

The Legend of George Washington and the Cherry Tree

Although most legends have some historical truth behind them, there are others that are completely made up. For example, the legend that tells about George Washington chopping down a cherry tree when he was a boy seems to have no basis in fact. It lasts, though, because people like to hear a story about a good act performed by a hero (*see* HEROES OR HEROINES), even if it is not true.

In this story, young George was practicing with a new hatchet, or ax. Soon he tired of practicing on logs from the woodpile. He wanted to try chopping down a real tree, so he cut down a fine young tree in his father's orchard. Then he looked more closely at it and realized it was a special cherry tree that his father had received from England, all the way across the Atlantic Ocean. George began to worry.

When George's father came home, he was angry to learn that his special tree had been chopped down. No one he questioned had any idea who had done the chopping. Finally, Mr. Washington came to George, who knew how angry his father was. Still, he took a deep breath and said, "Father, I cannot tell a lie. I cut down the tree. I am sorry." George's father replied, "I am sorry too. But I would rather lose all the trees in my orchard than have you tell a lie or be afraid to tell the truth."

The moral, or lesson, of this legend is that honesty is always the best policy.

events or HEROES OR HEROINES. Usually, there is some truth to a legend. For example, historians believe KING ARTHUR existed in real life, but as the legend about him developed, he began to appear larger than life. Generally, but not always, a legend has less to do with the supernatural than a MYTH does.

A legend may come down through the generations in prose or in a poetic form, such as in the ballad or folk song (*see* BALLAD AND FOLK SONG). For example, FRANKIE AND JOHNNY is a legend in ballad form.

In all parts of the world today, legends continue to form, often around sports figures, and the public

From "Rip Van Winkle" *by Washington Irving*

"I was myself last night, but I fell asleep on the mountain, and they've changed my gun, and every thing's changed, and I'm changed, and I can't tell what's my name, or who I am!"

The bystanders began now to look at each other, nod, wink significantly, and tap their fingers against their foreheads. There was a whisper, also, about securing the gun, and keeping the old fellow from doing mischief. . . . At this critical moment a fresh likely woman pressed through the throng to get a peep at the graybearded man. She had a chubby child in her arms, which, frightened at his looks, began to cry. "Hush, Rip," cried she, ". . . the old man won't hurt you." The name of the child, the air of the mother, the tone of her voice, all awakened a train of recollections in [the old man's] mind.

"What is your name, my good woman?" asked he.

"Judith Gardenier."

"And your father's name?"

"Ah, poor man, his name was Rip Van Winkle; it's 20 years since he went away from home with his gun, and never has been heard of since—his dog came home without him; but whether he shot himself, or was carried away by the Indians, nobody can tell. I was then but a little girl."

. . . The honest man could contain himself no longer.—He caught his daughter and her child in his arms.—"I am your father!" cried he—"Young Rip Van Winkle once—old Rip Van Winkle now!—Does nobody know poor Rip Van Winkle!"

talks about some people being "legends in their own time." [*See also* ABRAHAM LINCOLN AS "HONEST ABE"; ANNIE OAKLEY AND HER GUN; BILLY THE KID'S ADVENTURES; CAPTAIN JOHN SMITH AND POCAHONTAS; CUSTER'S LAST STAND–TWO VERSIONS; DANIEL BOONE'S EXPLOITS; DAVY CROCKETT AND THE ALAMO; EL DORADO; ELVIS, THE ONCE AND FUTURE KING; JESSE JAMES; JOHNNY APPLESEED; KING ARTHUR; ONEIDA MAIDEN SAVIOR; OUR LADY'S LITTLE GLASS; ROBIN HOOD; ROLAND'S LAST STAND; SHOOT-OUT AT THE OK CORRAL; THE SICK MAN'S GHOST.]

The Legend of Sleepy Hollow ❧

See IRVING, WASHINGTON (1783–1859).

Leprechauns ❧ *See* FAIRIES.

Literary Folktale ❧

Literature that has many similarities to a standard FOLKTALE but was written down by the author instead of existing for years only in the spoken form. As a result, a literary folktale stays the same from generation to generation.

Little Red Riding Hood ❧

A FOLKTALE of the FAIRY TALE type that warns children to obey their parents. The story goes back hundreds of years to the Middle Ages in Europe.

The Original Story. In the original, oral version, the little girl was sent by her mother to carry food to her ill grandmother, who lived in the woods. The little girl met a werewolf, a person who has been changed into a wolf, and told him where she was going. The werewolf got to the grandmother's house before the little girl and killed the grandmother, whom he chopped up and later served to the little girl. Then the

An illustration by Arthur Rackham of Red Riding Hood and the wolf dressed as a grandmother.

"Lon Po Po": *Like and Not Like* "Little Red Riding Hood"

A Chinese story that is older than LITTLE RED RIDING HOOD also tells about a wolf who tries to trick little girls.

"Lon Po Po" began as the mother was going to visit the grandmother, leaving at home three daughters: Shang, Tao, and Paotze. The mother told the girls not to open the door for anyone. Soon, a wolf tricked the girls into opening the door by saying he was Po Po, their grandmother. The wolf blew out the candle and got into bed with the girls. The girls quickly realized they had made a mistake. The voice they heard was lower than their grandmother's, and the foot they touched in bed was furry and had sharp claws.

Shang, the most clever girl, knew she had to get the wolf out of the house, so she suggested the girls pick gingko nuts at the top of the tree. Then Shang tricked the wolf into getting into a basket, which she and her sisters pretended to pull up so that the wolf could get nuts too. When the basket got very high, the girls let go, and the basket crashed to the ground, killing the wolf. The girls then went back into the house and fell asleep.

werewolf made plans to attack the girl, but she was clever and managed to save herself.

The Written Story. When the story was written down in 1697 by a Frenchman named Charles Perrault (*see* PERRAULT, CHARLES), he changed it in at least two ways. First, the wolf eats the grandmother. Second, the little girl cannot save herself. So in this version, the wolf eats the little girl, and the story ends very unhappily.

More than a hundred years later, the GRIMM BROTHERS, two Germans, wrote down the story in yet another way. In this version, a hunter arrives and becomes a hero (*see* HEROES OR HEROINES) by cutting open the wolf's belly to save both the grandmother and Little Red Riding Hood.

The Lesson. The version of the story that is most often told to English-speaking children is the one by the Grimms. At the very end of that story, the little girl realizes she got in trouble because she did not obey her mother, who told her to go straight to her grandmother's and not to dawdle or to talk to anyone along the way. The girl remembers that she spoke to the wolf and stopped to pick flowers. Her final words are, "I will never again wander off into the forest as long as I live, if my mother forbids it."

Ma Barker (1872–1935) ❧

An American woman who became a LEGEND because of her connection to an outlaw gang. With George Barker, whom she left in 1927, she had four sons: Herman, Fred, Arthur ("Doc"), and Lloyd. The first three were known by the gang name *Bloody Barkers*.

According to the FBI, Ma Barker planned the gang's crimes, which mostly involved kidnapping and robbing payroll offices, post offices, and banks in the 1920s and 1930s. The FBI claims to have tracked her down in Florida in 1935, where, in a gun battle, FBI agents shot and killed her and her son Fred.

However, a gang member's report, quoted in *Myths, Legends, & Folktales of America*, says that Ma Barker was not smart enough to set up a robbery. One way or the other, Ma Barker gained fame because of Americans' fascination with gangsters—and, perhaps, with mothers.

Magic Objects and Wizards ❧

In a MYTH, FAIRY TALE, FOLKTALE, or LEGEND, things and characters that can make the impossible happen. The magic may involve transforming something or someone into something or someone else.

One of the most well-known magic objects, the magic wand.

Aladdin's Magic Lamp

"Aladdin and the Wonderful Lamp" is a FOLKTALE in the book called ONE THOUSAND AND ONE NIGHTS, or *Arabian Nights*. Here is a short version of the story.

Aladdin, who lived in Arabia, was the lazy but honest son of a poor widow. He was sent into an underground cave by a magician who pretended to be Aladdin's uncle. Aladdin's job was to bring back a special lamp that was hidden in the cave. The lamp was an oil lamp—not the kind that works by electricity. Aladdin found the lamp, and he also loaded his pockets with beautiful gems that he found in the cave, so he was unable to hand the lamp up to his "uncle." The angry man sealed Aladdin and the lamp in the cave.

Aladdin, miserable and frightened, wrung his hands and, to his surprise, released a genie from the ring that the magician had given him. By using magic, the genie freed Aladdin from the cave. Then Aladdin learned that the lamp itself was magic. Whenever Aladdin rubbed the lamp, a powerful genie appeared to grant Aladdin's wishes.

Eventually, he married the daughter of the sultan, or ruler, of Arabia. Aladdin had a happy life with more wonderful adventures.

Magic Objects. To make some magic objects work, the owner must recite special words, which may be called a *charm* or *spell*. Such magic objects include wands, or sticks (often used by fairy godmothers, as in CINDERELLA), mirrors (as in "Snow White and the Seven Dwarfs"), and lamps and carpets (as in the story of Aladdin in ONE THOUSAND AND ONE NIGHTS).

Wizards. Wizards are magicians. They can be good or evil. Females who can do magic are called *sorceresses* instead of wizards. Certain wizards may also be gods. Some gods are born knowing how to do magic, but others must learn how to make magic happen.

An example of a wizard from folklore is Merlin in tales about KING ARTHUR. In contemporary literature, wizards appear in *The Wonderful Wizard of Oz* and in the Earthsea Quartet by Ursula LeGuin. [*See also* FAIRIES.]

Marwe in the Underworld

A tale from Kenya in Africa about disobedience, love, jealousy, dying, and coming back to life. These themes are common in folklore.

The Story. Marwe and her brother were supposed to keep the monkeys out of the bean fields. But they did not pay enough attention to their job, and the monkeys ate all of the beans. Fearing her parents, Marwe drowned herself and went to the Underworld, also known as the Land of the Dead. After many years, an old woman there used magic to decorate Marwe with jewels and to clothe her with beautiful robes. Then the old woman told Marwe that Sawoye was the best man in the world and sent Marwe home. Back in life, Marwe decided to marry Sawoye even though he had terrible skin. After their marriage, Sawoye's skin healed, and Sawoye became the most handsome man of all!

Many people were jealous of Marwe and Sawoye for their happiness and wealth. Neighbors killed Sawoye, but Marwe knew how to bring him back to life. Then Sawoye killed the neighbors. Marwe and Sawoye lived the rest of their lives happily and died without fear.

Matthew, Mark, Luke, and John

A GAME RHYME for counting out. Some counting-out rhymes are used to pick the person who will be "it" for a game such as hide-and-seek. Other counting-out rhymes are used to eliminate players until there remains only one—the winner. Whoever the leader is pointing to when he or she gets to the end of the rhyme is "it" or is out.

The men's names in the title, "Matthew, Mark, Luke, and John," are the names of the four biographers of Jesus in the New Testament of the Bible. They became Christian saints. No one knows for sure why their names were chosen for a game rhyme. Perhaps the reason is that a player can make a catchy rhythm by saying the four names in this order. Here is the whole rhyme:

> Matthew, Mark, Luke, and
> John
> Saddle the cat and I'll get
> on,
> Give me the switch, and I'll
> be gone,
> Out goes he!

The word *switch* in the third line means "stick or rod used for whipping an animal." [*See also* IBBITY, BIBBITY.]

Maui Fishes Up the Land

A story about a character who is part god and part human trickster (*see* TRICKSTERS). He has some but not all of the powers of a god. Stories about Maui come from Polynesia, islands in the central and southern parts of the Pacific Ocean.

One tale tells about the time Maui went fishing with his brothers. All the brothers except Maui spent each day fishing in order to bring food home to their families. Maui had not fished at all. He spent his time making a magic fish hook out of the bone he had tricked his grandmother into giving him from her jaw. When he was ready to fish, he needed bait to attract a fish. When his brothers refused to give him bait, Maui hit himself in the nose to start bleeding. Then he put some of his blood on the magic fish hook and started fishing.

The Maori people of New Zealand finish this story by saying that Maui caught the land they now live on and brought it to the surface of the sea. In fact, these people call New Zealand "The Fish of Maui."

Mayan Flood

A story told by the Maya people in their sacred book *Popol-Vuh*. The Maya had a rich civilization in Mexico and Central America until about the year 1000.

According to this story, God was not satisfied with his first two attempts to make human beings. None of the people he had made obeyed and loved God. Therefore, he sent in a great flood to destroy the people.

Then God tried again. First he sent parts of himself to the world, and these parts had two sons to help move the Sun and the Moon. Finally, it was time to make four men and four

The Mayans had many gods. Here is a very old sculpture of their rain god.

women out of yellow and white corn that he had ground. But when these people came to life, they could see too much, so God made another change and limited how far people could see. At that point, he was satisfied with his creation. Then God made dawn for his people, and the sun rose.

Other Creation Stories. The story that the Maya tell about creation and the flood are both like and unlike stories from other cultures, or groups of people. Like the story of GREEK CREATION, the Mayan story involves a supernatural power that is greater than human power. Unlike the story of NOAH'S FLOOD, the Mayan story shows God admitting that he had made mistakes that he must correct.

Mike Fink and the Deacon's Bull

An unusual TALL TALE about a frontier LEGEND—a storyteller who admits he did not win.

An animal showing its wild side just as the Deacon's bull did.

Mike Fink, a real person who lived from 1770 to 1823, worked as a boatman on the Ohio and Mississippi rivers. He did win a lot of fights but probably exaggerated his stories about them so that listeners would enjoy them more.

According to "Mike Fink and the Deacon's Bull," Mike was minding his own business when the unfriendly beast tried to attack him. Mike did not want to yell for help. He came up with the idea of staying out of the bull's way by hanging on to the bull's tail. Then he tried to escape the bull by climbing into a tree, but this plan backfired because the tree held a nest of large stinging insects. Mike dropped out of the tree and onto the bull's back. He hung on until they reached a fence, which Mike went flying over. He crashed on to the other side. One observer is supposed to have said, "Mike Fink has got the worst of the scrimmage once in his life."

Fighting and Bragging. Up until the Civil War began in 1861, Americans fought a lot and boasted about those fights they won. Maybe listeners enjoyed these stories because daily life on the frontier meant one struggle after another. In any case, many of the reports were not about people wanting to hurt others. Instead, they were about people, such as Mike Fink, being able to hold their heads up and say, "I gave it my best shot." Sometimes, though, the fights did involve people hurting each other— for instance, white men being cruel toward other groups of people, such as American Indians and African Americans.

Momotaro's Story
An ancient Japanese FAIRY TALE that, like European fairy tales, includes talking animals, elements of fear and danger, the triumph of good over evil, and a happy ending.

A child came to live with a poor, elderly, and childless couple, who raised him as their son. They named him Momotaro, or Peach Boy, because his mother had found him inside a huge peach in the river. When Momotaro was 15, he got permission from his father to fight the demons, which are like devils, on a faraway island. On his way to the island, Momotaro met a dog, a pheasant, and a monkey, all of whom joined him.

With the help of his companions, Momotaro killed many of the demons, and finally the demon king gave up. The boy freed some maidens who had been held as prisoners and, with treasures from the island, returned to care for his elderly parents.

Monsters ✦ *See* AMERICAN INDIAN FOLKLORE; FEARSOME CRITTERS; GLOOSCAP SLAYS THE MONSTER; IROQUOIS FLYING HEAD.

Moral ✦ *See* FABLE; PANCHATANTRA; PARABLE; THE POOR MAN AND THE SNAKE; PROVERB.

Mother Holle ✦ A FAIRY TALE from the GRIMM BROTHERS about a hard-working girl and a lazy girl who are stepsisters. The hard-working girl accidentally dropped a tool down the well from which her family drew water. Her WICKED STEPMOTHER demanded that the girl get the tool. After climbing into the well, the girl found herself in a beautiful land. There she gladly helped with baking bread, shaking down apples, and doing housework for a woman named

The lazy daughter gets her reward.

Mother Holle. Later, Mother Holle showered the girl with gold, a fitting reward, and sent her home.

The lazy girl also wanted a reward. Her mother told her to find the beautiful land. When she found it, she refused to work. She, too, got a fitting reward—but not the one she expected. [*See also* THE TALKING EGGS.]

Myth ✦ A story that tells how people feel about life or explains something about the world—for example, how the world was created or why an animal has a certain feature. In ancient times, some forces of nature were mysterious or frightening, so people needed to come up with explanations for the mysteries, including the mysteries of human life. Because myths deal with questions such as "Why are we here?" they are usually important in the religions of the world.

Myths almost always include one or more HEROES OR HEROINES who have special powers that go beyond those of an ordinary human being. Myths also usually involve gods or goddesses.

Makers of Myths. When people first created myths, they passed them on by word of mouth, so the myths changed over time. Later, people wrote down the myths, so the stories began to stay the same as time passed. But even today there are different versions of most myths. Some versions are simple, some are more complicated, and details of a story may vary from one version to another.

The makers of myths have lived all over the world. Each culture has its own myths. Sometimes, different groups have different explanations for the same element in nature. Sometimes, though, different groups have similar explanations.

A Myth: "Seneca Earth Diver"

Many American Indian tribes have myths about how Earth was formed. Here is a version of the myth by the Seneca Indians, one of the tribes that made up the Six Nations League of the Iroquois. The Senecas now live in the Northeast.

At one time, there was only water and sky—no land. Some animals, such as Turtle and Toad, lived in the water. Some people lived in the sky with the Great Chief. The sky had trees.

One day, the chief's daughter became ill. Following the advice of a man who had a dream, the chief placed his daughter next to a tree and then dug up the tree. Another man, angry about the tree, kicked the girl into the hole.

The girl started falling through space toward the water. The birds helped the girl by putting her on Turtle's back. Then they told Toad to dive into the water and bring back soil to make Earth on which the girl could live. The girl lived on Earth and had a baby. Later, people made Earth bigger.

Native American Folklore ❧ *See* AMERICAN INDIAN FOLKLORE.

Never Hold Your Head Too High

❧ An American FABLE that teaches people a lesson about the danger of boasting that they are better than others. In this fable, the characters are animals that can talk.

According to this short story, a small rooster criticized a goose for the way she went around a fence. In particular, the rooster did not like the way the goose ducked her head to get under the fence. The rooster was sure that when the goose bowed her head to get under the fence, she was saying, "I am ashamed of myself. I feel inferior, not as good as the other birds." Then the rooster showed the goose the way *he* would get around the fence. He climbed up to the top of the fence, holding his head very high. Before he had a chance to drop down on the other side of the fence, a large hawk flew by. The hawk grabbed the rooster by the feathers on his head and went off to have a good meal. So maybe the rooster did not know so much after all!

The Nightingale ❧ A FAIRY TALE by Hans Christian Andersen (*see* ANDERSEN, HANS CHRISTIAN) about kindness.

A nightingale, much like the loyal bird in the fairy tale by Hans Christian Andersen.

A nightingale is a bird that is known for its beautiful song. This particular nightingale, many people thought, was the most wonderful bird in the empire. The emperor, who wanted the best of everything, imprisoned the bird in the palace, where he could always listen to it. Soon, however, the emperor received a mechanical bird and sent away the real bird. Years later, when the emperor was dying, he wanted to hear the nightingale's beautiful song, but the mechanical bird was broken. The real bird returned out of loyalty and made the emperor well with his beautiful music. [*See also* LITERARY FOLKTALE.]

Noah's Flood 🐾 A bible story about how humans were punished for their sins but then given another chance to be good.

The Punishment. According to this Hebrew story, God thought the people who came after his creation of ADAM AND EVE were wicked. One of the bad things God saw among his people was violence. He therefore became sorry for making humans in the first place and decided to send a flood of high waters to destroy all of the humans and animals on Earth.

Saving Noah and a New Covenant. God indeed wanted to kill the living creatures, but he did not want the world to be without people and animals forever. He wanted new people and animals to live after the old people and animals died in the flood. Because a man named Noah had been good, God decided to save him, his wife, his three sons, and their three wives. God also decided to save two of each kind of animal. According to his plan, after the flood, new people and new animals would be born from the ones who had been saved. In time, the world would again be filled with people and animals.

God directed Noah to build an ark, or large boat, for his family and

Noah and the others leave the ark after the flood.

for the animals. God told Noah how to keep the ark safe when the rains came and gave him one week to get ready. Then God made it rain for 40 days and 40 nights, and as he planned, all the people and animals except those on the ark drowned. After the flood, when the world was dry again, Noah built an altar to worship God, who promised he would never send another flood to destroy the world. This promise that God made to Noah is called a *covenant*. [*See also* BIBLE STORIES; MAYAN FLOOD; WYOT FLOOD.]

Odysseus ❧ *See* TROJAN HORSE.

Oedipus and the Riddle of the Sphinx ❧ A MYTH from ancient Greece about a man named Oedipus and the sphinx, a creature that was part woman and part animal.

At the time when Oedipus is said to have lived, the sphinx was eating innocent people, because they could not answer her RIDDLE. The riddle asked, "Who walks on four feet in the morning, two feet at noon, and three feet in the evening?" Oedipus figured out that the answer is "a person," and the angry sphinx jumped off a cliff, killing herself. Everyone called Oedipus a hero (*see* HEROES OR HEROINES) and thought him worthy to marry the queen, whose husband had died. The mar-

riage did not bring happiness, however, because, unknown to Oedipus, the queen was his own mother, from whom he had been taken as a baby.

Ogres ❧ *See* FEARSOME CRITTERS.

Old Man Coyote and the Buffalo
❧ An American Indian story that is like a FABLE because it ends with a moral, or lesson. Like a fable, the characters in this story are talking animals.

Coyote the Trickster. Many different American Indian tribes have stories about Coyote, who is a trickster (*see* TRICKSTERS), meaning that sometimes he plays tricks on others and sometimes gets tricked himself. As a trickster, Coyote often causes trouble but sometimes helps people too. This particular story about Coyote is from the Shoshone Indians.

Coyote Becomes a Buffalo. The story explains that Coyote had grown old and missed running around all the time. When he saw a young buffalo, he felt great envy that the other animal was so handsome and so strong. Coyote complimented the buffalo, hoping that it would then change him into a young, beautiful animal. Indeed, the buffalo agreed to help. He went on to say very clearly that Coyote would look like a young buffalo but would not have the real buffalo's magic powers.

After Coyote took on the shape of a young buffalo, his life became very good. But a time came when another old coyote wanted Buffalo-Coyote to turn *him* into a young buffalo too. When Buffalo-Coyote tried to use magic powers, he did not always get the result he expected. The fable ends with the moral, "So always remember, don't start anything unless you know you can finish it." [*See also* COYOTE, IKTOMI, AND THE ROCK.]

Oneida Maiden Savior ❦ An

American Indian tale about a heroine (*see* HEROES OR HEROINES). It is fitting that a tale about a heroine comes from the Oneida. In the Oneida tribe, women owned the longhouses in which several families lived. Another sign of the women's importance is that the Oneida stressed the mother's side of the family in talking about ancestors.

The Legend. The LEGEND tells how some Oneida escaped an enemy raid and hid in a cave on a cliff. The problem they faced was not having food. They could either stay in the cave and starve to death, or leave, search for food, and fall into the enemy's hands. When the warriors met in council, a young woman named Aliquispo (sometimes given as Aliquisipo) said she had received a message from the spirits telling her to die in order to save her people.

Aliquispo explained her plan. First, she would pretend she was looking for food and let the enemy find her. Then she would agree to lead them to the cave, but instead she would bring the enemy to a space where her people could crush them with rocks.

Just as Aliquispo had planned, the enemy warriors found her and asked where her people were hiding. Aliquispo did not tell right away. After all, she did not want the enemy to become suspicious. So she let the enemy threaten her with fire. Then she told the enemy that she would lead them to the cave. At night, she brought the enemy warriors to the space below the cliff, and she made them all come close so that she could whisper directions. The warriors gathered around her, and she immediately called in a loud voice, "My people, destroy your enemies." The warriors killed the maiden, but the rocks come pouring down on them. The enemy never again attacked the Oneida.

The story ends with the belief that woodbine, a natural medicine, came from Aliquispo's hair and that honeysuckle, which the Oneida call "blood of brave women," was also a gift from the maiden savior.

One Thousand and One Nights

❧ Very old Persian, Indian, and Arabian stories collected over many years and published in English for the first time in the 1800s. In the early days, the stories had been told only by word of mouth, or by what is known as oral literature.

The Frame Story. The individual stories in the collection, as explained later, are famous. Surrounding all these stories is another story, called a *frame story*, about a young woman named Scheherazade. She married a sultan who hated women so much that, after marrying a woman and spending one night with her, he has her murdered the next morning and goes on to marry another woman. Scheherazade did not want to die and had a clever idea for saving herself.

The idea is that on the first night, Scheherazade would start telling a story but would finish it the next morning. The sultan would want to know how the story ended, so he would let Scheherazade live one more night. When the second night came, Scheherazade finished the first story but started another one, and, once again, she would not finish it by dawn. Once again, the sultan delayed her death. Scheherazade's plan worked. The pattern of interrupted storytelling continued for a thousand and one nights. By then, the the sultan felt such great love for Scheherazade that he no longer wished her to die.

Some of Scheherazade's Stories. Among the now-famous stories that

Maxfield Parrish (1870–1966) created this illustration for *One Thousand and One Nights.*

Scheherazade narrated are "The Seven Voyages of Sinbad," ALI BABA AND THE FORTY THIEVES, and "Aladdin and the Wonderful Lamp" (*see* MAGIC OBJECTS AND WIZARDS). These stories, like so many more in the collection, tell about exciting adventures and magic objects. Like the sultan, readers are enchanted by the stories and must find out how each ends.

Because the stories are not like other more religious Islamic stories, they are not an important part of Islamic literature, but they are still very popular.

Our Lady's Little Glass

A LEGEND written by the GRIMM BROTHERS to praise the Christian Saint Mary, called the Virgin Mary or, sometimes, Our Lady. The legend also explains the name of a flower.

The story tells that a wagon got stuck in mud. The driver became upset because he needed to deliver his wine. Mary came along and told him she would help free his wagon if he would give her some wine to drink. "Gladly," said the driver, "but I have no glass to put your wine in." Then Mary picked a white flower with red stripes. She showed the driver that the flower looked like a glass. He filled it with wine. When Mary drank the wine, the wagon got free of the mud. In some places, people still call that flower "Mary's Glass."

Juan Diego and Our Lady of Guadalupe

In the 1500s, Europeans brought their religions to North and South America, where Indians had lived and practiced their own religions for a long time. Sometimes the Indians put their older religious stories together with the newer European stories. Here is one such story that is still heard today.

In December 1531, an Indian named Juan Diego was on his way to a church. Up on a hill, he saw a dark-skinned woman. She said she was the Virgin Mary and would help the Indian people if the bishop would build a holy place on the hill.

At first, the bishop did not believe Juan Diego when he talked about a dark-skinned Virgin Mary. But then Our Lady of Guadalupe, as people called her, showed the bishop he should believe Juan Diego. The bishop built a holy shrine, which many people still visit. Many Spanish-speaking people in the United States have paintings of the Dark Virgin in their homes and pray to her.

Panchatantra ✌ A collection of Indian stories that go back to 200 B.C.E. Most of the stories in the collection are fables (*see* FABLE), in which animals act like human beings, and the listener or reader learns a moral, or lesson. The original *Panchatantra* was in an ancient language called *Sanskrit*. Today, the collection has been translated into 50 different languages, including English.

Arrangement of Stories. The stories in the *Panchatantra* are divided into five separate books. One is called *The Loss of a Friend*. Its 30 fables are about a jackal, a lion, and a bull that are having trouble getting along. Another book is called *The Winning of Friends*. It tells about the friendship of a crow, a mouse, a turtle, and a deer. The third book, called *Crows and Owls*, tells about a war between the two different kinds of birds. The fourth book, *Loss of Gains* has 12 tales. The most famous story in this book is called "The Ass in Tiger Skin". The fifth book is named *Ill-Considered Action* and has 11 stories. Many of the Indian tales in the five books of the *Panchatantra* later changed, either a little or a lot, and were told in many countries besides India.

"The Donkey in Tiger Skin." This story in the *Panchatantra* is very much like a story in an earlier collection of fables by AESOP. A young donkey wanted to be a tiger, so he made his parents get a tiger skin for him to wear. When he put on the tiger skin, he fooled some people into thinking he really was a tiger. Real tigers attacked him, and he dropped his tiger skin. As he ran away, people laughed and threw things at him. The moral of the story may be, "You cannot pretend you are someone else. You are who you are."

Parable ✌ A brief story that teaches a lesson. A parable is like a FABLE, because both a parable and a fable teach a moral, or lesson. But a parable is different from a fable, because the characters in a fable are animals who act like human beings, whereas the characters in a parable are truly human. Examples of parables are "The Prodigal Son" and THE GOOD SAMARITAN, which come from the Bible. [*See also* BIBLE STORIES.]

Paul Bunyan and Babe ❧

An oversized folklore hero (*see* HEROES OR HEROINES) and his oversized ox. Paul Bunyan was known by the nickname "King of the Lumberjacks." His main job was to chop down trees and get them to a sawmill, where they would be cut into wood for building, furniture making, and so on.

History of Paul Bunyan. Some folks say that men started talking about a huge lumberjack like Paul Bunyan in the early 1900s and that a Detroit newspaper wrote about him around 1910. Others say that no one talked or wrote about Paul Bunyan until an advertising writer for a lumber company made up a character with that name and wrote stories about him to help sell lumber from 1914 to 1916. Whatever the beginning was for Paul Bunyan, many stories have been told about his life, as well as about his animal companion, Babe the Blue Ox. According to some reports, people are making up stories about those two to this day!

Feats of Paul and Babe. Stories that make up the LEGEND about Paul Bunyan stress two things: his strength and his appetite. To give an idea of Paul Bunyan's strength, one TALL TALE says that Paul was very upset about losing Babe the Blue Ox in a gambling bet, so he dragged his ax across the flat land and made the Grand Canyon. On the topic of Paul's appetite, another tall tale says that to grease his huge grill, seven boys would skate across it with fatty hams strapped to their feet.

Babe the Ox was so long, according to tall tales, that Paul needed to use binoculars to see what the ox's hind legs were doing. Paul also needed four tons of grain to feed Babe at one meal. [*See also* DAVY CROCKETT AND THE ALAMO; JOHN HENRY; JOHNNY APPLESEED; PECOS BILL.]

Pecos Bill ❧

A hero (*see* HEROES OR HEROINES) of the American folklore category called TALL TALE. Pecos Bill was named in honor of the Pecos River in Texas. The river is near the place where he fell off his family's wagon and got left behind when he was still a baby. The baby survived and grew, because he was taken in by some caring coyotes. Pecos Bill was stronger than most grown men when, at the age of 13, he began to demonstrate his amazing skills.

One of Pecos Bill's first feats was taming a mountain lion. He was

One of Pecos Bill's first feats was to tame a mountain lion.

the only man who was able to stay on the lion's back, and finally the lion agreed to let Pecos Bill ride him. Another time Pecos Bill made a lasso out of live snakes and used it to bring down a bull.

In addition to getting the upper hand with ferocious animals, Pecos Bill could control other overwhelming natural forces. For instance, when he wanted to bring water from the Rocky Mountains down to his spread in New Mexico, he simply dug a river, which is now called the *Rio Grande*. At another time, Pecos Bill controlled a tornado by grabbing onto it and riding it until it finally gave up and turned into nothing more than a rainstorm.

Inventing Pecos Bill. Most characters in tall tales come out of the imaginations of ordinary people sitting around and making up stories to tell each other. But Pecos Bill was not invented that way. Instead, it seems that a newspaper writer named Edward O'Reilly made up the character and wrote stories about him. Soon afterward, people started talking about Pecos Bill and making up more stories about him. [*See also* DAVY CROCKETT AND THE ALAMO; JOHN HENRY; JOHNNY APPLESEED; PAUL BUNYAN AND BABE.]

Perrault, Charles (1628–1703) ❧

A Frenchman best remembered for collecting and retelling stories that belong to the category FAIRY TALE. Later, the tales were translated into English. Before Perrault wrote his versions, the fairy tales had existed only in spoken language.

Perrault's collection was first titled *Tales of Past Times, with Lessons* (1697) but later became known as *Tales of Mother Goose*. The book includes such favorite tales as CINDERELLA, PUSS IN BOOTS, SLEEPING BEAUTY, and LITTLE RED RIDING HOOD.

Pixies ❧ *See* FAIRIES.

Pocahontas ❧ *See* CAPTAIN JOHN SMITH AND POCAHONTAS.

The Poor Man and the Snake ❧

From AFRICAN AMERICAN FOLKLORE, a FABLE, which is a brief story that involves an animal and teaches a moral, or lesson. In most fables, the lesson is for an animal character, who represents a human being. But in this fable, the two human characters, the poor man and his wife, are the ones who misbehave and are taught the lesson.

The Story. A snake met a poor, hard-working man and offered to give him money (*see* HELPFUL ANIMALS). The snake had one rule that the man had to follow: he must never tell anyone, not even his wife, where the money came from. However, the man could not keep the secret. Once he told his wife that the snake had given him the money, bad things began to happen. The wife, who could not leave well enough alone, wanted more money, so she came up with a mean way of getting it. The husband followed her orders, hurt the snake, and came to a horrible end himself.

At the end of the fable, the storyteller states the moral, "Anyone who goes back on his promise and tries to harm the person who has done him a favor is sure to meet up with big trouble."

How "The Poor Man and the Snake" Is Like Another Folklore Story. This story from the African American culture is similar to a

Snakes are an important symbol in many cultures. American Indians cut this snake design onto a shell.

story from Germany called THE FISHERMAN AND HIS WIFE. Even though these two stories come from different parts of the world, they have something in common. In both stories, a character is not satisfied with what she has and wants more. The characters are also punished for being selfish.

Princes or Princesses ❧

Characters who often appear in a MYTH or a FAIRY TALE about a long-ago time and a faraway place. Usually, a prince or princess appears as ideal, or perfect. He or she has beauty, wealth, youth, and charm. Sometimes, though, it is not so easy for other characters to see these qualities. For example, WITCHES or wizards (*see* MAGIC OBJECTS AND WIZARDS) may change a prince into a monster or an animal who can become human again only when a princess loves him for himself (*see* BEAUTY AND THE BEAST). Or a princess may be under a spell or appear dead, and only the kiss of a loving prince can break the spell or bring the princess back to life (*see* SLEEPING BEAUTY).

Most myths or fairy tales read today focus on a prince rather than a princess. It is usually a prince, not a

This illustration by Arthur Rackham is for "The Frog Prince," another fairy tale that deals with a magic spell.

princess, who must leave home and go on a long journey or must face a number of tests before he can win the

A Princess from the Grimm Brothers: "The Goose Girl"

Here is a short version of this tale.

A widowed queen sent her daughter, the princess, off to marry a prince who lived far away. The queen sent a lady-in-waiting to serve the princess along the way and in her new home. But on the journey, the servant overpowered the princess. When the two arrived at the king's palace, the servant, wearing the princess's clothes and riding on the princess's horse, convinced everyone that she was the one sent to marry the prince. In the meantime, the princess, now dressed as a servant, was afraid to tell the truth. The king sent her off to work with the boy who cared for the geese.

Time passed, and word about the girl got back to the king. He learned that the head of a dead horse spoke to her. He learned that she could make the wind blow the boy's hat around. Finally, he found out the truth. He brought the real princess to the prince and punished the servant for her lies.

prize: marriage to a perfect person. In some cases, as in "The Princess and the Pea," the young woman does have some work to do. She must prove she really is a royal princess.

Proverb ❧ A saying that contains a truth about the experience or lives of human beings. Often a proverb is defined not only as a saying but as a *clever* saying. It may be clever because it rhymes or uses language in another interesting way. Some proverbs sound like ordinary speech—that is, they are folksy, as if created by ordinary people. Other proverbs sound more poetic, as if created by a very well educated person. Here are examples.

An apple a day keeps the doctor away. (*This proverb rhymes and sounds folksy.*)

You can lead a horse to water but you can't make him drink. (*This proverb does not rhyme, but it has a balance. First it says what you can do, and then it says what you cannot do. It also sounds folksy.*)

An eye for an eye and a tooth for a tooth. (*This proverb also has a nice balance. It sounds more poetic than saying, "If you do something wrong to me,*

I'll do something wrong to you.")

Early to bed and early to rise makes a man healthy, wealthy, and wise. (*In addition to rhyme, this proverb has a strong rhythm.*)

Many times the moral, or lesson, that appears at the end of a FABLE is a proverb. For example, at the end of OLD MAN COYOTE AND THE BUFFALO, the moral sounds like a proverb:

So always remember, don't start anything unless you know you can finish it.

Puss in Boots ❧ A story about a clever cat that helps his poor master become a wealthy man. This is one of the HELPFUL ANIMALS stories that has been called both a FOLKTALE and a FABLE. A popular version was written by Charles Perrault (*see* PERRAULT, CHARLES), but many other versions are known.

The cat, wearing boots, caught rabbits and other small animals, which he sent to the king as gifts. The cat told the king that the gifts were from the wealthy Marquis of Carabas, the made-up name the cat gave his owner. Through more tricks (*see* TRICKSTERS), the cat convinced the king that the rich and generous

Puss dresses up to serve his master.

Jason and his Argonauts sailed in the waters off Greece.

"marquis" deserved to marry the king's daughter.

The Quest for the Golden Fleece

❧ A long, ancient Greek poem that tells of a man named Jason, who makes a dangerous journey on a sailing ship called the *Argo*. Jason and the Argonauts, as his warriors are called, receive help from a god and a goddess. They travel from Iolcos to Colchis and back to Iolcos. In Colchis, Jason performs fearsome tasks and leaves with the golden fleece, or wooly coat, of a sacred, flying ram (a male sheep).

On this journey, Jason has many other adventures. One adventure involves the Harpies, horrible winged monsters. Later, he battles fierce women warriors called Amazons. Along the way, Jason and his men also survive the Clashing Rocks, which try to prevent the ship's passage.

The Quest for the Holy Grail ❧

A story handed down by Christian LEGEND and earlier by Irish and Welsh MYTH. This story, which in different forms has made its way into written literature around the world,

In earlier versions of Arthurian legend, it is Parsifal, or Sir Percivale, who is the only knight to achieve the holy grail.

tells about the search by knights for a sacred cup, dish, or goblet.

According to legend, Jesus Christ drank from the grail at the last supper. The legend goes on to say that when Jesus was crucified, some of his blood dripped into the grail, which Joseph of Arimathea was holding. The legend says that Joseph took the grail to England, where, by a miracle, it provided him with food and drink.

Later tales about KING ARTHUR tell of knights searching for the Holy Grail, which had disappeared, because people had become evil. According to these tales, a knight had to be pure to find and see the grail. One such pure knight turned out to be Galahad, the son of Lancelot, one of King Arthur's greatest knights. When Galahad was allowed to look into the grail, he was carried up to heaven.

Today, the term *grail* sometimes refers to any object for which someone has been searching a long time. [*See also* MAGIC OBJECTS AND WIZARDS.]

Raven Steals Fire for People

A MYTH of a tribe of American Indians from what is now the northwestern United States and western Canada. The tribe's name is Quillayute (also spelled Quileute and Kwakuitl), which may mean "beach at the north side of the river" or "smoke of the rivers."

The myth tells that Raven brought daylight and fire to the people. Up until the time of the story, daylight and fire had been hidden from the people by a powerful being named Gray Eagle. Raven was a handsome man, but when he fell in love with Gray Eagle's daughter, he changed himself into a snow-white bird in order to please the young woman. Indeed, she liked the bird and asked him to stay in her father's lodge.

From the lodge, Raven stole the Sun, the Moon, stars, fresh water, and fire. He put the Sun, the Moon, and stars in the sky so that people would have daylight as well as night-

A raven with black feathers. This myth tells how the feathers became dark.

time. He spilled the water on the ground to create all the rivers and lakes. Then he had to drop the fire, because it was burning his beak and making his feathers black. He dropped the fire onto rocks. It is said that when people saw the fire come out of the rocks, they learned how to make their own fire by rubbing two rocks together.

Riddle

A word puzzle that asks a listener or reader to answer a question or to identify what is being described. The puzzle contains a clever trick or wordplay to throw the listener or reader off the track. Often, as soon as the listener or reader gives up and is told the answer, he or she realizes how obvious and simple the solution is and immediately wants to challenge someone else to figure out the answer.

People have been telling riddles for thousands of years. For example, both the ancient Greeks and the ancient Japanese made up riddles. Sometimes, two very different cultures, or groups of people, tell very similar riddles.

Usually, a riddle stands alone, but at times—as in BIBLE STORIES or a Greek MYTH—it may be part of a longer story. For example, the ancient Greeks had a myth about the sphinx, a creature that was part woman, part dog or bull, and part lion, dragon, and bird. The myth about the sphinx includes a riddle that the creature would ask. [*See also* THE BAKER'S DOZEN; CONTEST OF RIDDLES; KNOCK, KNOCK; OEDIPUS AND THE RIDDLE OF THE SPHINX; RIDDLES—A COLLECTION.]

Riddles—A Collection

The group of riddles (*see* RIDDLE) presented by Kemp P. Battle in his anthology called *Great American Folklore: Legends, Tales, Ballads and Superstitions from All across*

Brer Rabbit's Riddle

Here is an example of a riddle that appears within a story.

Brer Fox wanted to get even with the trickster (*see* TRICKSTERS) Brer Rabbit, so the fox asked the rabbit to climb a tree and pick some peaches. The fox planned on grabbing the rabbit when he climbed out of the tree backward. But the rabbit was smarter than the fox and saved himself.

While he was in the tree, the rabbit posed the following riddle to the fox, but the fox could not solve it.

> The big bird rob and the little
>   bird sing,
> The big bee zoom and the little
>   bee sting,
> The little man lead and the big
>   horse follow,
> Can you tell what's good for a
>   head in a hollow?

The rabbit then said that if the fox would eat some honey, he would be able to solve the riddle. The next thing he knew, Brer Fox found himself with a hive of bees over his head—thanks to Brer Rabbit.

America. Battle found a lot of material in books and articles written by other people who collect folklore. In addition, Battle traveled through the countryside of America, where he himself heard and wrote down tales, jokes (*see* JOKE), sayings, and riddles. Here is a sampling of the riddles from his book.

Some riddles contain a direct question, as in the following two. (The answer to each riddle is given in parentheses.)

> If a man was born in Eng-
>   land,
> Raised in Kansas,
> And died in Beijing,
> What is he?
> > (Answer: dead)

> Sisters and brothers have I
>   none,
> But that man's father is my
>   father's son.
> Who am I?
> > (Answer: a man telling
> > of his son)

Other riddles simply describe something or give statements about an object, and the listener or reader has to figure out what the teller of the riddle has in mind.

> Round as a saucer, deep as
>   a cup,
> Yet the whole Mississippi
>   couldn't fill it up.
> > (Answer: a strainer)

> The longer she stands, the
>   lower she grows.
> > (Answer: a candle)

Ride a Cockhorse

A GAME RHYME in which a child is placed on an older person's knee and moved up and down while the following words are recited to the rhythm of a trotting horse.

> Ride a cockhorse to Ban-
>   bury Cross,
> To see a fine lady upon a
>   white horse;
> Rings on her fingers and
>   bells on her toes,
> And she shall have music
>   wherever she goes.

A *cockhorse* is another name for a rocking horse, and *cross* refers to a crossroads, or a place where two roads cross each other.

Robin Hood

A character in British folklore. For centuries, people have argued about whether Robin Hood was a real person of the twelfth and thirteenth centuries and, if so, who he was—an ordinary man or a nobleman—when and where he had been born, and when and how he died. Without knowing the truth, people started making up and singing ballads about Robin Hood (*see* BALLAD AND FOLK SONG). Then, in 1495, the first printed book about Robin Hood appeared. Many others followed. In the nineteenth century, an author named Howard Pyle wrote *The Merry Adventures of Robin*

Hood especially for children. There have been other modern versions and a number of movies as well.

Robin Hood's Traits. Over time, the character Robin Hood grew and became more famous. Most important, Robin Hood, as he has come down to the twenty-first century, is an outlaw hero (*see* HEROES OR HEROINES)—an *outlaw* because he steals from the rich and a *hero* because he gives to the poor. Robin and his band of Merry Men—including Little John, Scarlock (or Scarlet), Much the Miller's son, Allen-a-Dale, and George-a-Green—live in Sherwood Forest in the north of England.

Besides disobeying the king, Robin and his men are always fighting with the sheriff of Nottingham and other powerful people who they think are corrupt or dishonest. In fact, in tales about Robin Hood, the rich from whom Robin and his men steal always seem to be bad or corrupt, whereas the poor people, whom they help, tend to be very good.

Changes over Time. The early stories about Robin Hood are more violent. The later stories include the topic of romantic love by introducing Maid Marian. These stories also introduce Friar Tuck. Of course, some things about Robin Hood stay the same over the centuries: as a man, he

Robin Hood was an expert with arrows.

is honest, generous, courteous, and religious.

Roland's Last Stand ❧ The story of the death of Roland, a legendary (*see* LEGEND) knight of supernatural strength and great honor. Roland supposedly lived in the late 700s. His story was written down in French around 1100 in an epic poem called *The Song of Roland*.

Roland was the nephew of Charlemagne, a powerful Christian ruler of people known as Franks. Roland thought it was his duty to protect Charlemagne and his troops, who were trying to get out of Spain and return safely to their own land. Roland, who was at the back of the Franks, was attacked by the Moors—people who were not Christians who were considered evil by Christians.

During this great battle, another man named Oliver urged Roland to blow his horn to make Charlemagne and his army return to help in the battle with the Moors. In response, Roland said that to call for help would bring shame on him, his family, and his countrymen. Only after the battle had raged for some time did Roland sound the horn. Charlemagne returned, but by that time, Roland, the last Christian on the battlefield, had died.

The Rooster, the Mockingbird, and the Maiden ❧ A FAIRY TALE

from the Hopi Indians. The story tells how two birds competed to make the sun rise in the morning. The winner would marry a beautiful maiden.

Up until this time, the rooster knew how to wake people, but only the mockingbird knew how to make the sun come up. So the rooster traveled to Moenkopi to ask the wisest

roosters and hens how to make the sun rise. To teach him, they sang songs and crowed all night. Finally, the sun came up. Then they sent the rooster home to hold the contest. Soon after, the mockingbird went to see his friend, the Great Thunderbird, to ask for his help in winning the contest.

That night, with the mockingbird watching, the rooster sang and crowed just as the wisest roosters

An illustration of Thunderbird, a character in "The Rooster, the Mockingbird, and the Maiden."

and hens had taught him. But the mockingbird's friend, the Great Thunderbird, opened his enormous wings and blocked the sun that was rising. It looked as if the rooster had failed.

The next night, with the rooster watching, the mockingbird sang and whistled. Then the sun came up. So the mockingbird married the beautiful woman.

This Hopi story ends by saying that later the mockingbird and his wife had children, who talked all the time just like their father. But the rooster, who found another wife, had children who were gentle and kind and did not talk so much.

Some people who hear the story ask, "In the end, who was happier—the rooster, who tried so hard, or the mockingbird, who cheated in the contest?" [*See also* FASTING FOR THE HAND OF THE QUEEN'S DAUGHTER.]

Rumpelstiltskin

A German FAIRY TALE in which an evil dwarf named Rumpelstiltskin helps a woman in order to get what he wants, but in the end he loses.

A beautiful young woman was given the impossible task of spinning straw into gold to save her life and marry the king. She did not know how to make gold, but Rumpelstilt-

This illustration by Arthur Rackham shows a "ridiculous little man . . . leaping, hopping on one leg, and singing."

skin did, and he promised to make gold for the woman if she would give him her first baby. When she married the king and had a child, the dwarf agreed to let her keep the baby only if she could guess his name, which he had never told her. But he made the mistake of singing his name in the forest, where someone overheard and told the queen. After she said his name, Rumpelstiltskin became so angry that he destroyed himself.

Sacred Story

Sacred Story ❧ A story, usually very old, that is central to a religion or culture. A sacred story may tell how the world came to be. All cultures have one or more such stories, called creation stories (*see* GREEK CREATION).

A sacred story may tell why something is the way it is. For example, HOW CORN CAME tells why the plant is yellow and green. In this sense, a MYTH is a sacred story.

Judaism and Christianity. Another kind of sacred story tells people how they should act. For example, the story "David and Goliath" (*see* BIBLE STORIES) suggests standing up for one's beliefs no matter the size of the enemy.

Islam. Just as the Bible is sacred to the religions Judaism and Christianity, so the Koran (or Qu'ran) is the holy book in the religion Islam. Some of the stories in the Koran are similar to those in the Bible—for example, the stories about Abraham and Jesus. But the Koran focuses on Mohammed as God's prophet.

Hinduism. The *Mahabharata* is an example of the sacred writings of the Hindu religion. It is an epic poem that may be the longest literary work ever written.

Allusions. Because sacred stories are so old and important, writers through many ages refer directly or indirectly to people and places in them. An indirect reference to a sacred story is an example of an allusion. For example, if in a TV script, one character calls another "Judas," the writer is alluding to the story of how Jesus was betrayed by his follower Judas Iscariot. Calling a person "Judas" is accusing that person of betraying a friend. [*See also* BUDDHA AND THE BODHI TREE.]

Santa Claus ❧ According to MYTH, the man who brings Christmas presents to children. Originally, Saint Nicholas, a special saint for children, was part of a European winter holiday. Later, Germans replaced Saint Nicholas with Kriss Kringle. Dutch settlers in America replaced Saint Nicholas with Sinter Claes, and then English settlers changed Sinter Claes to Santa Claus.

Children are told that Santa lives at the North Pole, where elves

This postcard Christmas greeting comes from the early twentieth century.

make toys. On Christmas Eve, flying reindeer carry Santa and the gifts around the world. He stops on rooftops, slides down chimneys, and puts gifts in Christmas stockings and under Christmas trees.

Shoot-out at the OK Corral ❧ A
gun battle that took place in October 1881 in Tombstone, Arizona. It has become part of the LEGEND of the Wild West.

The Players. The gunfight started with a threat by the outlaw Ike Clanton to kill the marshal, Wyatt Earp, and the dentist, Doc Holliday. Clanton rounded up four other outlaws to be on his side, and they took their positions at the corral. Helping Wyatt and Doc were two other Earps, Virgil and Morgan.

The Shoot-out. At least one written version of the legend says that Wyatt Earp planned not to shoot unless the outlaws shot first. Reports claimed that two men on Clanton's side did fire their guns first. Witnesses said that the whole battle lasted less than a minute.

The marshal's side had better shooters and was more deadly than Clanton's side. During the short contest, Clanton panicked. Grabbing hold of Wyatt's arm, he said, "Don't kill me, Wyatt! Don't kill me! I'm not shooting." Later, when Doc complained that Wyatt missed the chance to shoot Clanton, the marshal explained, "He wouldn't jerk his gun."

Justice. Before, during, and after the shoot-out, the sheriff, Johnny Behan, did not stand up for the law. In fact, he tried to hurt the marshal. But at the end of the story, the good guys not only won the battle but also were found innocent by a grand jury.

The Sick Man's Ghost ❧ A nineteenth-century American LEGEND that tells of one of the many beliefs that people at that time had in

supernatural powers. The supernatural involves actions that are impossible for ordinary human beings, animals, and objects.

The Story. When some people thought they had seen a person who was known to be dead and buried, they said that they had seen a ghost (*see* GHOSTS AND GOBLINS). Other people claimed that a ghost would appear shortly *before* a person died.

According to "The Sick Man's Ghost," a young man, sometime after the Civil War, was walking home from a dance in a pioneer settlement. The young man had to pass a farm where a very sick old man lived. In the field was another figure. The young man thought the figure was the old man's son and started to approach him. But then the figure passed over a fence not by climbing or jumping but by *floating* off the ground. The legend says that the old man's cattle had also seen the figure rise and had become frightened.

Later the young man's boss explained to the young man that the sight was the ghost, or spirit, of the sick old man. The appearance meant that the old man would soon die. In fact, the old man died a few days later.

Ghosts Today. Tales such as "The Sick Man's Ghost" were common in America during pioneer days. Even in today's world of science and technology, some Americans still love stories about ghosts or other supernatural beings. Some popular ghost stories have been written by Stephen King. The movie called *Ghostbusters* was also a hit.

Simple Simon

A FAIRY TALE by Hans Christian Andersen (*see* ANDERSEN, HANS CHRISTIAN) about a silly, or "simple," brother who wins a prize that his two educated brothers fail to win.

The two smart brothers and Simon each wanted to marry the king's daughter. She had announced that she would marry the man who was the best at speaking up. Simon rode a goat and carried a dead crow, an old wooden shoe, and mud to the palace. His brothers laughed at him. But after the smart brothers both failed to please the princess, Simon did an excellent job of talking with her. The story closes with, "So in the end Simple Simon became king, with a wife of his own and a crown and a

Simon, looking silly, tries to buy a pie from a pieman at the fair.

throne." It also ends with a warning that the story may not be true.

Before Andersen wrote the tale about Simple Simon, the character showed up in a children's poem that begins with the following lines:

Simple Simon met a
    Pieman
Going to the fair.
Says Simple Simon to the
    Pieman,
"Let me taste your ware."
Says the Pieman unto
    Simon,
"First give me a penny."
Says Simple Simon to the
    Pieman,
"I have not got any."

The poem goes on to show Simon doing foolish things but making people laugh along the way.

Sleeping Beauty ❧ A FAIRY TALE

that is not only frequently read to children but is also the basis for a movie by Walt Disney and a ballet by Marius Petipa to music by Peter Tchaikovsky.

The story was written down by an Italian storyteller in 1634, but the versions by the French writer Charles Perrault (*see* PERRAULT, CHARLES) and the German GRIMM BROTHERS are more famous. (The Grimms called their story "Brier Rose.")

The Familiar Story. At a party celebrating the birth of a princess (*see* PRINCES OR PRINCESSES), one

The prince approaches the sleeping princess in an illustration by Jennie Harbour.

fairy (*see* FAIRIES), angry because she had not been invited, placed a curse on the baby. She said that at the age of 15, the princess would prick her finger on the spindle of a spinning wheel and die. Another fairy changed the curse so that instead of dying, the princess would fall into a hundred-year-long sleep, to be awakened only by the kiss of a prince.

All the spinning wheels in the kingdom were removed. However, when the princess turned 15, she came across an old lady in the palace who had one, and pricked her finger. She—and everyone else in the palace—fell into a deep sleep. Only when a hundred years had passed was a prince able to wake the princess—and, of course, they married and lived happily ever after.

Snow White ❧ *See* WICKED STEP-MOTHER.

Spider Grandmother Leads the People

❧ A MYTH that the Hopi people of the Southwest tell about a supernatural being, or goddess. This story is about the work that Spider Grandmother (Kokyanwuuti) did to bring people into the place that the Hopi call the Fourth World.

Getting to the Fourth World. The myth says that in the the beginning there were no animals and no people. There was Tawa, the Sun spirit, or god, who created the First World, which contained only creatures, such as insects. Tawa was not happy with thes creatures, who carried on wars, so he sent Spider Grandmother to lead them to the Second World. Along the way, the creatures turned into dogs, wolves, and bears. These creatures disappointed Tawa also, for they did not value life. This time Tawa sent Spider Grandmother to lead the creatures to the Third World. Along the way, they turned into people. In the Third World, the people learned a lot, but many became evil. So now Spider Grandmother told the people who were still good to leave the Third World and go to a world that the hummingbird had told them of—a world above the sky called the Upper World.

With prayers and ceremonies, the chief and his wise men made a swallow, a dove, a hawk, and a catbird. Only the last could fly through the opening in the sky that led to the Upper World. The catbird brought back a message that the Upper World would indeed be the new home for people. But the people needed a way to climb through the opening. After trying to climb up many plants, the people, with help from Chipmunk and Spider, used a hollow bamboo reed, which grew all the way up to the opening and beyond. Led by Spider Grandmother, the people climbed through the bamboo reed to the Fourth World, where they live today.

Other Stories about Spider Grandmother. Other tribes have different stories about Spider Grandmother. For example, the Cherokee tell how Spider Grandmother brought fire to the people. In other parts of the Southwest, Spider Grandmother appears as Thinking Woman. Still other tribes call her Changing Woman.

Spiritual ❧ *See* AFRICAN AMERICAN FOLKLORE; BALLAD AND FOLK SONG; JOHNSON, JAMES WELDON.

Stagolee and the Sheriff

❧ A TALL TALE that grew out of a LEGEND about a real black man named Stacker Lee. This man was an outlaw whom people either loved or feared. He got away with breaking the law.

The original story, in the form of a ballad (*see* BALLAD AND FOLK SONG), tells that Stagolee killed a man named Billy Lyons for stealing his hat. Stagolee claimed that the hat was magic (*see* MAGIC OBJECTS AND WIZARDS). It allowed him to change his appearance.

A modern version of the story by the folklore collector Julius Lester still includes magic. In this version, Billy Lyons was angry at Stagolee for beating him at a card game, so Lyons knocked off Stagolee's hat and spit in it. No matter what Lyons said or did next, Stagolee would not forgive him. Then Stagolee shot Lyons dead.

The First Sheriff. The sheriff was very upset that Stagolee always got away with his crimes, so he planned to arrest Stagolee. The men who worked with the sheriff knew better and ran the other way. Then the sheriff met Stagolee in a bar and jabbed a pistol into his ribs. But Stagolee threw the sheriff across the room and shot him dead.

The Second Sheriff. The second sheriff planned to kill Stagolee when he was drunk and asleep by putting a rope around his neck. Stagolee woke up and challenged the sheriff to go ahead and hang him, which the sheriff did. But half an hour later, Stagolee was still alive, so the people cut him down and sent him back to bed. From that point on, the sheriff left Stagolee alone.

Stepmother ✌ *See* WICKED STEP-MOTHER.

Stormalong ✌ A legendary hero (*see* HEROES OR HEROINES) of sea adventures. Stormalong was the captain of a ship called the *Courser*. According to one TALL TALE, the ship was so gigantic that it would not fit through the English Channel unless Stormalong coated the sides of the ship with soap. Another tall tale tells how the Panama Canal between North and South America was created. It explains that during a hurricane, *Courser* hit the coast of Central America hard enough to break the two continents apart.

The cowboy on horseback is still an important part of American folklore.

The Streets of Laredo ✌ A popular American folk song (*see* BALLAD AND FOLK SONG) about the death of a cowboy. The first and last stanzas are the words of someone who had once known the cowboy and then came across the cowboy's body in Laredo, Texas. The other five stanzas are spoken by the cowboy himself. He explains that he died from drinking and gambling. He claims, "I'm a young cowboy, and I know I've done wrong," but he also sounds proud of his life when he says, "Oh, bury me beside my knife and my six-shooter, / My spurs on my heel, my rifle by my side."

Two lines in the song talk about a drum and a fife, a musical instrument like a flute. Those two instruments were played when burying a soldier in England or Ireland but not when burying a cowboy in America. It turns out that the song, with many different words but the same melody, goes back to 1790 in Ireland. Like much folklore, this song traveled to another country and changed over time. But even though many words from nineteenth-century life in the American Old West were added to the song, the drum and fife remained from the Irish version.

Superman ❧ A superhero created in the United States in the 1930s. Superman first appeared in comic strips, then comic books, a television series, and finally several full-length movies. Even though Superman is a

creation of the twentieth century, he displays some of the elements found in myths (*see* MYTH) from long ago and far away.

The Qualities of Myth. Superman, like some heroes (*see* HEROES OR HEROINES) in myths, was born in another world (Krypton) and then abandoned. Also like a classic hero, Superman has enormous strength and supernatural powers. He takes on the responsibility of protecting his city (Metropolis) on Earth from evil forces even if he has to disguise himself (as Clark Kent, reporter) to do so. Like some gods or godlike heroes, Superman has a weak spot (Kryptonite can hurt him) and, at least in recent stories, can feel love (for Lois Lane).

A color poster depicting Superman vs. Atom Man.

The Talking Eggs
A FOLKTALE from the southern part of the United States about two sisters, one good and one bad. Unfortunately, their mother is blind to the good daughter's sweetness and to the bad daughter's meanness.

The Good Sister. The sweet girl's name was Li'l Tater. No matter what she was asked to do, she did it without complaining. For example, if she was told to get water from the well, she would drag the heavy bucket there and back, singing to herself all the while. She always did good deeds. For example, when she heard an old woman in the woods begging for some water, she shared her water.

Once the bad sister, Blossom, was so mean to Tater that the good sister ran to the woods and began to cry. The old woman appeared and said, "You come wid me awhile." Tater went with the old woman into a bush that opened into a whole new world. Although Tater saw strange things, she did not laugh at or insult the woman, and she did everything the woman asked. The next day, the old woman told Tater to gather eggs from the chicken coop but only the eggs that said, "Take me." Tater obeyed, even though the eggs that said, "Don't take me" were covered with jewels. Tater was to throw the eggs over her shoulder on her way home. She obeyed again and was rewarded by rich treasures that popped out of the eggs.

The Bad Sister. When Blossom, the bad sister, saw Tater's treasures, she went to the old woman. But when Blossom saw strange things in the woman's world, she laughed and said mean things. Then Blossom took the jeweled eggs, but when she threw them over her shoulder, horrible things popped out of them instead of treasures. [*See also* MOTHER HOLLE.]

Tall Tale
A story that is so far-fetched, stretched, or exaggerated that a listener or reader cannot believe it even though it is told as if it were true. Most, but not all, tall tales are supposed to be humorous.

Like other forms of folklore, many American tall tales began as stories shared by word of mouth. As time passed, some of these tales were written down. Then some people decided to write and publish original tall tales, ones that had *not* started out as oral stories. [*See also* PAUL BUNYAN AND BABE; TWAIN, MARK.]

Teasing Rhyme ❧ A GAME RHYME

that people, usually children, say when they want to make fun of someone or to hurt someone's feelings. Sometimes children make up an original teasing rhyme, but most of the time, they simply repeat a teasing rhyme that they have heard some-

one else say. Some teasing rhymes last for many generations. Here are a few examples.

> Ink, ink
> A bottle of ink,
> The cork fell out
> And you stink!

> 2 and 2 are 4,
> 4 and 4 are 8,
> 8 and 8 are 16,
> Stick your nose in
>   kerosene!

> Fiddledy, diddledy, dee,
> I see something you don't
>   see!

A Tall Tale: "Davy Crockett Meets His Match"

Here is a summary of a TALL TALE about not one but two folk heroes (*see* HEROES OR HEROINES).

Mike Fink (*see* MIKE FINK AND THE DEACON'S BULL) worked as a boatman on the Ohio and Mississippi rivers. Davy Crockett (*see* DAVY CROCKETT AND THE ALAMO) was a hero of the backwoods. Each man considered himself the best gun shooter around. When Fink boasted to Crockett's face, the woodsman challenged the boatman to a shooting match.

First, Crockett fired his long rifle and shot the ears off a cat 150 yards away. Fink responded by shooting the tails off a faraway sow and her little pigs. Then he asked

Crockett to put the tails back on. Crockett laughed at this demand, saying that it was "onpossible," but he pointed out that Fink had left about an inch of tail on one of the pigs. Crockett cooly took aim and shot off the rest of the tail.

At this point, Fink got mad. He turned to his wife and shot half a comb off the top of her head. Next, he invited Crockett to shoot off the other half. Crockett declined. He said that if he pointed a rifle at a woman, his hands would shake and he would injure her for sure.

Although Crockett let Fink win this battle, maybe he won the war by showing that he was more of a gentleman.

Look, look,
You dirty crook,
You stole your mother's
Pocketbook!

When a child has been hurt by a teasing rhyme, he or she may answer back with the following rhyme or something like it.

Sticks and stones
May break my bones,
But words will never hurt
    me!
When I die,
Then you'll cry
For the names you've
    called me!

Theseus Goes to His Father ❧

A MYTH about a young hero's (*see* HEROES OR HEROINES) worthiness. Raised by his mother, Aethra, in the south of Greece, Theseus had never known his father, Aegeus. But Aegeus had said that when Theseus was old enough and strong enough to lift a rock under which he would find a sword and a pair of sandals, it would be time for him to go to his father in Athens and become the rightful heir to the throne. At the age of 16, Theseus lifted the rock and traveled to Athens, carrying with him the sword and the sandals.

When Theseus arrived in Athens, the king's wife, who was the sorceress Medea, tried to murder the young man. But when the king saw the sword that Theseus carried, he knew that Theseus must be his son and banished his wife.

Like a true hero, Theseus had not taken the easiest route to Athens. Instead of making a short sea voyage, he had chosen to go by land and beat down villains and bandits along the way. One of his victims was the robber Procrustes ("The Stretcher"). This robber tortured people by cutting off parts of their bodies or stretching their bodies to fit his bed. When Theseus, on his way to Athens, captured Procrustes, the hero put the robber through the same horrible torture for which Procrustes was famous. Only when Theseus had completed such heroic deeds against villains did he present himself to his father.

Thousand and One Nights ❧ *See* ONE THOUSAND AND ONE NIGHTS.

Till Eulenspiegel and the Beehive ❧ A FOLKTALE from Germany about a peasant who outsmarts two thieves. The peasant is the hero (*see* HEROES OR HEROINES) of this tale and of many other German folktales too.

At the beginning of this tale, Till had gone to the fair and was tired from playing and drinking. In a farmyard, he found a beehive that looked like a basket made of twigs. He crawled in, closed the top of the basket, and fell asleep.

Two thieves hunting for honey came along and stole the beehive with Till inside. As they carried the beehive, it swayed so that Till woke up and heard the two men talking. Till peeked out and then reached out with his hand to pull the hair of the thief walking in front. That thief complained to the other thief. A little later, Till again reached out and this time he pulled the hair of the thief walking in back. Now the second thief complained to the first thief. The two thieves put the beehive down and chased each other. Till had some peace and quiet, so he went back to sleep in the beehive until morning.

The Tortoise and the Hare ❧ A

FABLE that teaches a lesson about concentrating and trying hard. The story, which tells of a race between the two animals in the title, was told in ancient times by AESOP and in the 1600s by La Fontaine.

The Characters. As with other fables, the main characters are animals who stand for human beings. One character is a tortoise, or a turtle, which is very slow-moving. The other character is a hare, which is like a large rabbit with long, strong back legs, so it can jump great distances and move swiftly.

The Contest. The slow tortoise said that he could beat the hare in a race to a tree in the distance. The swift hare laughed at the tortoise, whom he knew he could beat easily. In fact, the hare was so sure of himself that he gave the tortoise a head start.

The tortoise and the hare, as drawn by Arthur Rackham for *Aesop's Fables.*

Then the hare went off to eat and nap. In the meantime, the tortoise put one foot in front of the other and slowly made his way toward the tree. When the hare woke up and saw that the tortoise was near the tree, he started hopping. But the hare was too late. The tortoise won the race.

The Lesson. The lesson, or moral, of this fable is, "Slow and steady wins the race." It means that a person who concentrates, tries hard, and keeps going, has a good chance of succeeding.

A Story about Ananse's Stories

Ananse the spider is one of the most popular TRICKSTERS in folklore. He appears in tales told by the Ashanti people from Ghana in Africa.

Ananse wanted to buy the sky-god's stories, so he asked their price.

"You must bring me Onini, the python; Mmoboro, the hornets; Osebo, the leopard; and Mmoatia, the fairy," said the sky-god.

"I will bring you those things," Ananse agreed, "along with my mother, Nsia."

Ananse asked his wife, Aso, "How can I catch the python?"

"Cut a branch from a tree, along with some creeper vine," Aso answered. "Pretend you want to measure the python's great length with the branch. Then tie him to the branch with the vine."

Ananse did as Aso said. Then he brought the python to the sky-god.

"How shall I catch the hornets?" Ananse asked Aso.

"Fill a gourd with water," said Aso. "Sprinkle the hornets to make them think it is raining. When they fly into the gourd to get out of the rain, trap them inside."

After Ananse brought the hornets to the sky-god, he asked Aso, "How shall I catch the leopard?"

"Dig a hole," she instructed him.

Ananse dug a deep hole and covered it. When the leopard fell into the hole, Ananse killed him with a knife and gave him to the sky-god.

Next, Ananse covered a doll with sticky tree sap. He put food in the doll's hands and left it on the ground. Soon a fairy (see FAIRIES) came, ate the food, and thanked the doll. Then she slapped the doll for not saying, "You're welcome." The fairy's hands stuck to the doll, and Ananse tied her up. He brought the fairy and his mother to the sky-god.

"Now all my stories are yours," the sky-god told Ananse. "We will call them spider stories." [See also BRER RABBIT AND TAR BABY.]

Tricksters ❧ Important folklore characters who use their wits to outsmart others. Sometimes animals, sometimes humans, sometimes a mixture of both, and usually male, tricksters often play the role of practical joker, clown, or cheat. Other times, tricksters serve as helpers to humans by teaching them new ways of living—for example, how to make fire. Sometimes, a trickster's cleverness backfires, and it is the trickster who gets tricked.

One example of the trickster in AMERICAN INDIAN FOLKLORE is Coyote. In a Crow Indian story, he makes people out of mud. In a Zuni Indian MYTH, he steals the Sun and the Moon, which escape and flee to the sky, where they remain. In COYOTE, IKTOMI, AND THE ROCK, Coyote gets tricked by a rock, although he survives in the end. [*See also* BRER RABBIT AND TAR BABY; GLOOSCAP SLAYS THE MONSTER; KRSNA STEALS THE CLOTHES; MAUI FISHES UP THE LAND.]

Trojan Horse ❧

According to LEGEND, the wooden horse the Greeks used to trick their enemy, the Trojans. In 1200 B.C.E., during a war between the Greeks and the Trojans, the Greeks came up with a trick: they built a huge, hollow, wooden horse and left it outside the walls of Troy. Then they pretended to sail for home. The Trojans, thinking the horse was a gift, brought it inside the city walls. That night, soldiers who had hidden inside the horse climbed out and opened the city gate. In marched the rest of the Greeks, and they destroyed Troy.

Today, the term *Trojan horse* is used to mean any unexpected way to attack an enemy from within.

Tsimshian Lullaby ❧

A folk song (*see* BALLAD AND FOLK SONG) from a tribe of American Indians of the Pa-

The Greeks hid in a giant wooden horse to trick the Trojans.

cific Northwest. Like people from many cultures around the world, the people of the Tsimshian tribe created special songs to help babies fall asleep, usually, by repetition.

This lullaby, like others, tells what a baby will do when she grows up. It contains the hopes of the older person who sings it. So in this way the song not only lulls the baby but also brings comfort to the adult.

The words say the little girl will pick berries, dig wild rice, and gather sap. Here is an English translation of part of the lullaby.

The little girl will pick wild
roses.
That is why she was born.

Twain, Mark (1835–1910)

The pen name of a famous American writer who was able to make a short story sound like a TALL TALE. Twain is known for his ability to capture in writing the sounds and rhythms of American speech. Examples of Twain's short stories include "The Celebrated Jumping Frog of Calaveras County" and "The Blue-Jay Yarn."

Twain's real name was Samuel Langhorne Clemens. The expression *mark twain*, meaning "two fathoms (12 feet) deep," was one Twain had heard in his youth while working on steamboats on the Mississippi River. [*See also* LITERARY FOLKTALE.]

Mark Twain in his later years.

from "The Celebrated Jumping Frog of Calaveras County" *by Mark Twain*

The following words are spoken by the character named Simon Wheeler.

Well, this-yer Smiley had rat-tarriers, and chicken cocks, and tomcats, and all them kind of things, till you couldn't rest, and you couldn't fetch nothing for him to bet on but he'd match you. He ketched a frog one day, and took him home, and said he cal'lated to educate him; and so he never done nothing for three months but set in his back yard and learn that frog to jump. And you bet you he *did* learn him, too. He'd give him a little punch behind, and the next minute you'd see that frog whirling in the air like a doughnut—see him turn one summerset, or may be a couple, if he got a good start, and come down flat-footed and all right, like a cat. He got him up so in the matter of ketching flies, and kep' him in practice so constant, that he'd nail a fly every time as fur as he could see him. . . .

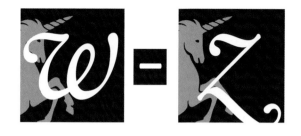

Waterjar Boy

Waterjar Boy ❧ A character in a MYTH told by the Tewa Indians of New Mexico. The myth bears similarities to many other myths. For example, as in other myths, the character has an unusual birth, goes in search of something, and makes a trip to another world.

The Birth. A woman at Skiyatki was making jars to hold water. Her daughter was helping her. The older woman went to get water. While she was gone, the younger woman was working on the clay with her feet. Somehow the clay got inside her and made her pregnant. When the young woman gave birth, her child was not a baby but a waterjar boy. Waterjar Boy grew and played with the other children, even though he didn't have arms or legs.

One day, Waterjar Boy was rolling alongside his grandfather. The two of them were out hunting for rabbits. Waterjar Boy rolled against a rock and broke open. Out stepped a handsome, well-dressed boy, who then introduced himself to his grandfather, grandmother, and mother.

The Search, or Quest. The boy went looking for his father, even though his mother told him that he did not have a father. The boy was sure he would find his father at a spring, and he did. The father took the boy into the spring, where they went into another world to see the father's relatives. Then the boy returned to this world.

More about the Other World. Soon the boy's mother died, so the boy went back to the spring to be with his father. There, his father told him that he had made the mother get sick and die so that the mother and the son could live with the father in the spring. Then the family stayed together.

Wicked Stepmother ❧ In a FAIRY TALE, after a mother dies, the evil character who marries the father and makes life miserable for his child—the hero or heroine (*see* HEROES OR HEROINES). Just as many heroes in folklore share characteristics, so do many stepmothers, who are presented in fairy tales as very bad people. Often the wicked stepmother wants to get rid of her husband's child in order to have all the man's money or attention for herself. Sometimes the stepmother has children of her own and sees the stepchild as getting in their way, or she may want the stepchild to act as a servant for her or her own children. The father, for some reason, never seems to notice the stepmother's wickedness until the end of the story, when he sends her away or helps to destroy her.

Perhaps stepmothers are shown to be evil because small children may see them as strange and different from the mothers they remember and love. In any case, in the world of fairy tales, goodness wins out over evil, and the child destroys, or at least escapes from, the stepmother. [*See also* CINDERELLA; MOTHER HOLLE.]

The Wicked Stepmother in "Snow White"

Snow White was the daughter of a beautiful queen and a king, but her mother died when she was born. The woman who then married the king was beautiful also, but she would not be satisfied until she was the *most* beautiful woman alive. When Snow White grew up into a beautiful girl, the new queen was very jealous of her.

The queen was not only envious, she was evil as well. She began to plot Snow White's murder. When Snow White managed to escape to safety with a band of dwarfs, the queen found out and tricked Snow White once, twice, three times until she managed to kill her.

The fairy tale has a happy ending, as fairy tales do. Snow White comes back to life and marries a prince. The stepmother comes to a horrifying—and very hot—death.

Witches   In the folklore of many cultures, women who have magical powers and are usually pictured as evil. Witches tend to appear at night, sometimes flying on broomsticks. They often wear black clothes, but they can change their entire appearance whenever they wish. They can also change humans into animals and affect the weather. Their homes may be huts in the woods, where they stir boiling cauldrons, or large pots, in which they prepare special potions and poisons. Animals that appear in stories with witches include cats, toads, and owls.

Although many stories tell about the evil that witches do, sometimes a witch can help one human being while harming others. For example, in THE QUEST FOR THE

Witches flying on broomsticks.

GOLDEN FLEECE, a beautiful witch helps Jason. *The Wonderful Wizard of Oz* is a story with a good witch as well as a bad one. [*See also* BABA YAGA TALE.]

Wizards
See MAGIC OBJECTS AND WIZARDS.

Wolf
See LITTLE RED RIDING HOOD.

Wyot Flood
A story told by the Wyot people, an American Indian tribe in what is now northwestern California. Their name is sometimes spelled Wiyot. As in NOAH'S FLOOD

"La Llorona," *or the Weeping Woman: A Witch? A Ghost?*

Stories about WITCHES and ghosts (*see* GHOSTS AND GOBLINS) are supposed to scare children and make them behave properly. The Hispanic FOLKTALE "La Llorona" is one of these stories.

The story has a few versions. In one version, a woman killed her babies because their father would not marry her. In another version, the woman did not kill the children, she only lost them. In another, the children died accidentally. But all the versions tell that the mother, dressed in white, roamed the world, crying, trying to get back her children. To stop their children from being bad, parents threatened that La Llorona would kidnap them to take the place of her lost babies.

The story "La Llorona" is believed to go back to an Aztec story that Spanish people heard when they arrived in Mexico hundreds of years ago.

and MAYAN FLOOD, this story tells that the creator was dissatisfied with the people who lived in the world. The Wyot called the creator Above Old Man. He wanted to wipe

A Native American Indian design of a flying bird similar to the one in "Wyot Flood."

Yankee Doodle ✒ A song (*see* BALLAD AND FOLK SONG) sung with pride by American soldiers during the Revolutionary War. People who study folklore have traced the song back and found out that the English doctor who wrote the words was actually making fun of the raggedy fighters who wanted independence from England. He was using the term *Yankee* to mock the New En-glanders. Folklorists also point out that the words of the song were then set to the tune of an English folk dance. Still, American soldiers liked brave Yankee Doodle, the character in this song, so they sang the words and tune anyway.

The words of the song that are most familiar are probably these:

Yankee Doodle went to
town
A-riding on a pony,
He stuck a feather in his
hat
And called it macaroni!

Yankee Doddle, keep it
up,
Yankee Doodle dandy!
Mind the music and the
steps,
And with the girls be
handy!

When the song was new, people made up additional stanzas, so that,

out the people with water and make new, better people for the world.

According to the Wyot story, Condor, a huge flying bird, knew that the flood was coming and prepared for it by weaving a basket so that he and his sister would survive in the water. They did survive, as did other birds, but no people existed after the flood. It was up to the birds to make new people. This time Above Old Man liked the people.

like a lot of oral folklore, the piece kept growing. Here are some of the stanzas that nowadays may be less familiar. They are reprinted from *Great American Folklore* by Kemp Battle.

> Father and I went down to
>   camp
> Along with Captain Good-
>   win,
> And there we saw the men
>   and boys
> As thick as hasty pud-
>   ding.
>
> There was Captain Wash-
>   ington
> Upon a slapping stallion,
> Giving orders to his men,
> I guess there were a
>   million.
>
> The troopers, too, would
>   gallop up
> And fire right in our faces,
> It scared me almost half to
>   death
> To see them run such
>   races.

Yankee Pedlar ❧ A FOLKTALE that paints a picture of the American traveling salesperson, who carried his merchandise from town to town before many stores opened. According to the folklore that was handed down, the traveling salesperson brought not only goods but also entertainment to town. For one thing, the salesperson knew how to tease cus-

tomers. When somebody wanted a new pair of boots, for example, the Yankee Pedlar looked around his cart until he found a pair of molds for making enormous candles. Then he would say, "Fit you like a whistle, sir."

The pedlar could also be entertaining when rattling off what was for sale. The list seemed never to end. Here's a sample:

> I've got most everything
> you ever heard tell on:
> essences, wintergreen,
> peppermint, lobely-tapes,
> pins, needles, hooks and
> eyes—broaches and
> brasslets—smelling bot-
> tles—castor ile—corn-
> plaster—
> mustard—garding
> seeds—silver spoons—
> pocket combs. . . .

The smarter men and women who listened to the pedlar tried to use good judgment and not fall for every product being sold. Even though the pedlar offered "patent pills, cure anything you like," it was not likely that the medicines worked. In trying to get good money for useless products, the pedlar was playing the role of a trickster (*see* TRICKSTERS).

Yeh-Shen ❧ A FAIRY TALE from China about a girl who is badly treated by her WICKED STEPMOTHER but, with the help of magic (*see* MAGIC OBJECTS AND WIZARDS), finds happiness.

The story is similar to but also different from CINDERELLA. It begins by saying that a long time ago, a chief had two wives. Each wife gave birth to a girl, but then one wife died, and so did the chief. Yeh-Shen, the baby who lost both parents, was raised by the wife who lived. This woman was jealous of Yeh-Shen's beauty and made her do all the hard chores.

Yeh-Shen's only friend was a fish.

Yeh-Shen's only friend was a fish. One day the stepmother tricked the fish, killed it, and ate it. When Yeh-Shen began to cry, a very old man appeared. He told her to save the fish's bones and to kneel before them whenever she needed help. Then the man flew off. Yeh-Shen saved the bones, and time passed.

At festival time, Yeh-Shen asked the bones for clothes so that she could go to the parties. The fish gave Yeh-Shen a beautiful dress and tiny golden shoes for her tiny feet. He warned her not to lose the shoes.

When Yeh-Shen did lose one on the way home from the festival, the fish's bones stopped talking.

A man found the shoe and sold it to a merchant, who presented it to a king. On seeing the tiny shoe, the king wanted to find its owner. He put the shoe on display, and Yeh-Shen took it home to return it to the bones. The king followed Yeh-Shen home. Kindly, he asked her to put on the shoes, and again she appeared in lovely clothes. Yeh-Shen and the king married. The stepmother and stepsister were crushed to death by stones.

Selected Bibliography

Ballads and Folk Songs

Lomax, Alan, ed. *Folk Song U.S.A.: The 111 Best American Ballads.* New York: New American Library, 1975.

Quiller-Couch, Arthur, ed. *The Oxford Book of Ballads.* Great Neck, N. Y.: Granger, 1979.

Sandburg, Carl. *The American Songbag.* New York: Harcourt, 1955.

Characters in Folklore

Anaya, Rudolfo. *Maya's Children: The Story of La Llorona.* New York: Hyperion, 1997.

Anderson, Bernice G., collector. *Trickster Tales from Prairie Lodgefires.* Nashville: Abingdon, 1979.

Bruchac, Joseph. *Heroes and Heroines, Monsters and Magic: Native American Legends and Folktales.* Freedom, CA: Crossing, 1998.

Curry, Jane Louise. *Robin Hood and His Merry Men.* New York: McElderry, 1994.

Dahl, Roald. *Roald Dahl's Book of Ghost Stories.* New York: Farrar, Straus & Giroux, 1983.

Faber, Doris. *Calamity Jane: Her Life and Her Legend.* Boston: Houghton, 1997.

Green, Carl R., and William R. Sanford. *Davy Crockett: Defender of the Alamo.* Berkeley Heights, NJ: Enslow, 1996.

Green, Roger Lancelyn. *King Arthur and His Knights of the Round Table.* New York: Puffin, 1995.

Hill, Kay. *More Glooscap Stories: Legends of the Wabanaki Indians.* New York: Dodd Mead, 1970.

Isham, Bruce. *Johnny Appleseed.* Tasmania, Australia: Bandicoot, 1998.

Kellogg, Steven. *Mike Fink: A Tall Tale.* New York: Morrow, 1992.

———. *Paul Bunyan: A Tall Tale.* New York: Morrow, 1984.

———. *Pecos Bill: A Tall Tale.* New York: Morrow, 1986.

Lehane, Brendan. *Wizards and Witches.* Alexandria: Time-Life, 1984.

Robinson, Gail. *Coyote, the Trickster.* New York: Atheneum, 1981.

Spies, Karen. *Our Folk Heroes.* Brookfield, CT: Millbrook, 1994.

Williams, Marcia. *The Adventures of Robin Hood.* Cambridge: Candlewick, 1995.

Wilson, Ellen. *Annie Oakley: Young Markswoman.* New York: Aladdin, 1989.

Fables

Bolliger, Max. *Tales of a Long Afternoon: Five Fables and One Other.* New York: Dutton, 1989.

Winter, Mio. *The Aesop for Children.* New York: Scholastic, 1994.

Fairy Tales

Andersen, H. C. *Hans Andersen's Fairy Tales.* Translated by L. W. Kingsland. Oxford: Oxford University Press, 1985.

———. *Tales and Stories.* Translated by Patricia L. Conroy and Sven L. Rossel. Seattle: University of Washington Press, 1980.

Chorao, Kay. *The Child's Fairy Tale Book.* New York: Dutton, 1990.

Grimm Brothers. *Grimms' Tales for Young and Old: The Complete Stories.* Garden City: Doubleday, 1977.

Grover, Eulalie Osgood, ed. *Mother Goose: The Classic Volland Edition.* Northbrook, IL: Hubbard, 1997.

Haviland, Virginia. *The Fairy Tale Treasury.* New York: Coward, McCann & Geoghegan, 1972.

Hearn, Michael Patrick, ed. *The Victorian Fairy Tale Book.* New York: Pantheon, 1988.

Jacobs, Joseph, ed. *English Fairy Tales.* New York: Reprinted by Knopf, 1993.

———. *Favorite Celtic Fairy Tales.* Reprint. Mineola, NY: Dover, 1995.

———. *Indian Fairy Tales.* Reprint. Mineola, NY: Dover, 1990

Lang, Andrew. *The Andrew Lang Fairy Tale Book: Forty-One Stories from around the World.* Edited by Michael Patrick Hearn. New York: New American Library, 1986.

Matthews, John, and Caitlin Matthews, eds. *A Fairy Tale Reader: A Collection of Story, Lore, and Vision.* London: Aquarian/Thorsons, 1993.

Perrault, Charles. *The Complete Fairy Tales of Charles Perrault.* New York: Clarion, 1993.

Folktales

Beck, Brenda E. F., ed. *Folktales of India.* Chicago: University of Chicago Press, 1987.

Cole, Joanna, ed. *Best-Loved Folktales of the World.* New York: Doubleday, 1982.

Dee Brown's Folktales of the Native American Retold for Our Times. New York: Henry Holt, 1993.

Forest, Heather. *Wisdom Tales from around the World.* Little Rock, AR: August House, 1996.

Glassie, Henry, ed. *Irish Folktales.* New York: Pantheon, 1985.

Renaux, J. J. *Cajun Folktales.* Little Rock, AR: August House, 1992.

Yolen, Jane. *Favorite Folktales from around the World.* New York: Pantheon, 1988.

Young, Richard. *African-American Folktales for Young Readers.* Reprinted by August House, 1997.

Legends

Brown, Dee Alexander. *Teepee Tales of the American Indian, Retold for Our Times.* New York: Holt, Rinehart and Winston, 1979.

Brown, Michael. *A Cavalcade of Sea Legends.* New York: Walck, 1972.

Bruchac, Joseph, and Jonathan London. *Thirteen Moons on a Turtle's Back: A Native American Year of Moons.* New York: Philomel, 1992.

Haviland, Virginia, ed. *Native American Legends.* New York: Collins, 1979.

Myths

Bierhorst, John. *The Mythology of Mexico and Central America.* New York: Morrow, 1990.

Bruchac, Joseph. *Native American Stories.* Golden, CO: Fulcrum, 1991.

D'Aulaire, Ingri. *D'Aulaire's Norse Gods and Giants.* Garden City: Doubleday, 1967.

———, and Edgar Parin D'Aulaire. *D'Aulaire's Book of Greek Myths.* Garden City: Doubleday, 1962.

Delacre, Lulu. *Golden Tales: Myths, Legends, and Folktales from Latin America.* New York: Scholastic, 1996.

Evslin, Bernard. *Heroes, Gods, and Monsters of the Greek Myths.* New York: Four Winds, 1966.

Farmer, Penelope, ed. *Beginnings: Creation Myths of the World.* New York: Atheneum, 1978.

Hart, Avery. *Ancient Greece! Forty Hands-on Activities to Experience This Wondrous Age.* Charlotte, VT: Williamson, 1999.

Keenan, Sheila. *Gods, Goddesses, and Monsters.* New York: Scholastic, 2000.

Low, Alice. *The Macmillan Book of Greek Gods and Heroes.* New York: Macmillan, 1985.

Mayer, Marianna. *Women Warriors: Myths and Legends of Heroic Women.* New York: Morrow, 1999.

McCaughrean, Geraldine. *The Crystal Pool: Myths and Legends of the World.* New York: McElderry, 1998.

———. *The Silver Tree: Myths and Legends of the World.* New York: McElderry, 1997.

Monroe, Jean Guard, and Ray A. Williamson. *They Dance in the Sky: Native American Star Myths.* Boston: Houghton, 1987.

Osborne, Mary Pope. *Favorite Norse Myths.* New York: Scholastic, 1996.

Philip, Neil. *The Illustrated Book of Myths, Tales, and Legends of the World.* London: Dorling Kindersley, 1995.

———. *Odin's Family: Myths of the Vikings.* New York: Orchard, 1996.

Rabin, Staton. *Monster Myths: The Truth about Water Monsters.* New York: Watts, 1992.

Rockwell, Anne F. *The One-Eyed Giant and Other Monsters from the Greek Myths.* New York: Greenwillow, 1996.

Shepherd, Sandy. *Myths and Legends from around the World.* New York: Macmillan, 1995.

Vinge, Joan D. *The Random House Book of Greek Myths.* New York: Random House, 1999.

Tall Tales

Erdoes, Richard. *Tales from the American Frontier.* New York: Pantheon, 1991.

Osborne, Mary Pope, and Michael McCurdy. *American Tall Tales.* New York: Knopf, 1991.

Page numbers for main entries (including feature box titles) are in boldface. Page numbers for illustrations are in italics.

Folktale